HIDDEN TALENT

UNCOVERING
WHAT REALLY MAKES
A CHAMPION A CHAMPION

TRAVIS DAUGHERTY

To Aden, Owen, and Leah

Never forget how much I love you,
how awesome you are,
and how much you're capable of.

TABLE OF CONTENTS

Part 3: YOUR HIDDEN TALENT

INTRODUCTION

There are some words we can all agree we love having attached to our name, our reputation, or our identity. One of those words is "champion." If you've ever been recognized as a champion, it's probably a positive memory you love thinking back on yourself or having someone else bring up. I doubt you've ever been offended by someone labeling you a champion in any important area of life.

If you haven't been a champion, or if you're pursuing the title again wherever you're working, practicing, and performing today, then you probably spend at least some of your time dreaming of the day you can earn or re-earn that label yourself. That's the dream that drives us to put in all the time and do all the work. It drives us to keep learning and improving. It's likely what's driven you to pick up this book. If that's what you're after, then I'm glad you're here.

So let's start at the beginning. If you want to be a champion, then it's worth clarifying…what makes a champion a champion? The truth is, it depends on how deep you're willing to dig. The easy answer – the obvious one – is that champions win. You don't have to dig real deep to uncover that truth. That's probably the image you create in your mind when you think "champion:" someone celebrating in the winner's circle, hoisting the trophy, and making the headlines. You see what's easy to see – the positive outcome or the

1

happy ending. On the surface, it's the easiest conclusion to come to: that champions win.

But if you're willing to dig deeper, you'll find that champions aren't who they are because they win. In fact, actually, just the opposite is true. Champions win because of who they are. Hall of Fame football coach Bill Walsh said, "Champions behave like champions before they are champions." That means beyond just what you see on the surface – the victories, the trophies, the headlines – you'll find that champions, in any area of life, have sown certain traits, certain attributes, and certain abilities into their being first, and *then* reaped the harvest of those traits, attributes, and abilities in the winner's circle after. This is true for you, too. You aren't a champion because you win. Actually, just the opposite is true. You win because you've done the hard work it takes to become a champion.

That process, of becoming a champion, is really about developing the gifts and talents you've been given in order to maximize your potential – to make you your winningest self. That word, "talent," is another one of those words we love having connected to who we are and what we do, isn't it? Like being a champion, the idea of being talented is fun and alluring. I doubt you've ever been offended by someone telling you they thought you were talented in any important area of life.

So in a culture where, more than ever, talent is enjoyed by those who have it and envied by those who don't, isn't it crazy to think we could ever manage to miss it? How could we possibly manage to neglect some of the gifts we should be most proud to possess? We're talking about gifts that, once recognized and developed, can set us apart. Gifts that can help us win. Gifts that can make us champions.

Uncovering this kind of talent – Hidden Talent, you might call it – is the purpose of this book. Of course, we all know from experience that talent is not evenly distributed. Some people may have gifts, either physically or mentally, that you don't have. That's a fair, and in some ways important reality to recognize.

But recognizing that reality isn't nearly as important as recognizing that there are also many gifts directly connected to becoming a champion in your line of work that you *have* been given, but maybe you've managed to overlook. If you're here, reading along with an interest in becoming a champion yourself, this should be great news: you have what it takes. In fact, each one of us does. I hope the deeper we dig here together, the more plainly you can see that usually in more ways than we'd like to think or maybe admit, becoming a champion is up to us.

It doesn't matter what shortcomings, weaknesses, or deficiencies you may have. It doesn't matter how little money you've got. It doesn't matter who your parents are, or how your DNA's constructed, or what challenging experiences you've endured in your past. You probably haven't been given every gift, but you've been given all you need to become a champion.

Of course, having all you need to become something isn't even remotely close to actually doing the work it takes to become that thing. "Becoming" is a process, and make no mistake, it does take work. Just as there is no biological or circumstantial disadvantage that can keep you from becoming a champion, there's no privilege or power that entitles you to it, either. It doesn't matter how much money you've got. It doesn't matter who your parents are, or how your DNA's constructed, or what good fortune you've experienced in your past. You can have every advantage that on the surface seems to set you up…and you can still fall short. Why? Because you aren't born a champion; you become one.

Wherever you're giving your time and energy today – in sports, at work, or at home – life is in many ways a game to be won or lost. Anywhere responsibility or opportunity exists, competition exists, too. It might involve the challenge of competing against someone or something else. More often and more importantly, it's the challenge you're facing against yourself and your own potential. However it looks, champions recognize the game that's being played. They recognize how winning is really defined and what exactly it takes to win. And then they step in the arena and compete.

I hope you can uncover, in the game you find yourself playing today, what really makes a champion a champion – to recognize how winning is really defined and what exactly it takes to win. Yes, as we've said already, champions win. But *why* do they win? If anyone is capable of becoming a champion, what is it that separates the champion from everyone else? Let's start by digging deeper into three simple things that champions do – three simple things you can do, too, to become a champion yourself.

CHAPTER 1:

CHAMPIONS CHASE EXCELLENCE

DO WHAT CHAMPIONS DO

It's easy to see that champions are driven. They are motivated and inspired. On the surface it might appear they're driven by the pursuit of success — that burning desire to be on top. That's the picture of the champion we created earlier — standing in the winner's circle, hoisting the trophy, making the headlines — the one standing above the crowd. But, you might be surprised to learn, the pursuit of success is not really what motivates a champion.

If you dig deeper, you'll see that for the champion, success is just one part of a larger pursuit. It's the glamorous, sexy part of the champion's story — the part that's easy to see and celebrate and aspire to — but it's also naïve, and maybe even a little bit dangerous, if you aren't willing to see the whole picture. Champions win, yes, but that result is simply the by-product of a bigger, deeper, more important endeavor. The champion isn't just pursuing success; the champion is chasing excellence.

This picture, the one of the champion chasing excellence, is more realistic and more complete. It does of course include some time in the winner's circle or with the trophy or in the headlines, because champions win. But chasing excellence is about more than just winning. While success is measured by an outcome or a result – one that's focused on comparing your performance with others – excellence is focused on the process of becoming the best *you* can be.

Pursuing success is usually easier, more comfortable, and more convenient than chasing excellence; that's why most people prefer it. But it isn't the most effective way to reach your full potential in any area of life, and – ironically – not even the best way to achieve those winning results so many of us are after. Champions recognize that a full commitment to running their own race, as well as possible every day, regardless of what anyone around them is doing, is the straightest path to excellence. Ironically, as a by-product of this pursuit, it's also the best way to achieve success.

So while the successful outcome is where the champion is recognized, it's the process, the journey – the pursuit of excellence – where the champion is made. While success is about celebrating the positive outcome or happy ending, excellence is about using whatever happens today, even if it isn't positive or happy, to improve for tomorrow. Success is about what we see under the spotlight on the big stage, when everyone's watching, but excellence is about what we do in the dark, when no one's watching. You need the spotlight and the stage to confirm someone as a success, but excellence isn't so picky. Excellence can be exhibited anywhere. In fact, whatever it is you're doing today, and wherever you find yourself doing it, it can be done like a champion.

So why then, you might be wondering, isn't everyone chasing excellence? Because chasing excellence is tough. It's rarely glamorous or sexy. Contrary to popular opinion, it can be downright ugly, awkward, or even painful. But this is a more complete picture of the champion's experience. It's the reality of the commitment the champion's made – a commitment to the whole story, not just to the highlights. Many have tried, but few have illustrated more clearly what this commitment looks like than President Teddy Roosevelt did in his famous speech, "The Man in the Arena." It's a perfect picture of the champion chasing excellence:

> "It's not the critic who counts; not the man who points out how the strong man stumbles, or where the doer of deeds could have done them better. The credit belongs to the man who is actually in the arena, whose face is marred by dust and sweat and blood; who strives valiantly; who errs, who comes short again and again, because there is no effort without error and shortcoming; but who does actually strive to do the deeds; who knows great enthusiasms, the great devotions; who spends himself in a worthy cause; who at the best knows in the end the triumph of high achievement, and who at the worst, if he fails, at least fails while daring greatly, so that his place shall never be with those cold and timid souls who neither know victory nor defeat."

Champions are the ones in the arena. Win or lose, they are the ones whose faces are marred by dust and sweat and blood, having given their very best to the competition they find themselves in today. Champions strive valiantly. They are enthusiastic and devoted; they've given their whole heart to this endeavor. Yes, they know the triumph of high achievement, because champions win. But, as Roosevelt points out, champions lose some, too, as part of their pursuit. They err. They come up short. They fail. In fact, champions fail just as much – and in some cases, maybe even more than everyone else, because they understand that failure isn't the opposite of excellence. Struggle and challenge and failure are *a part* of excellence. Champions fail, yes, but fail while daring greatly. Then they learn from the experience, dust themselves off, and get back in the arena to go at it again.

While the champion is in the arena, the loser is not. That word, "loser," can have a harsh connotation, and in many cases – sometimes even here – it's harshness is warranted. Most of the time in this book, however, you'll see that term used not so much to describe a complete idiot or total bum, but instead someone who's simply losing that game that's being played today – maybe by falling short of success, but more likely and more importantly, by accepting something short of excellence.

As is often the case, the reality of what something is gets clearer by holding it up next to its opposite, and a loser is simply what a champion is not. Defining each gets easier standing next to the other. So if the champion is the man in the arena, as Roosevelt said, the loser is outside, watching and probably criticizing. The champion is striving valiantly; the loser surrenders easily. The champion, win or lose, is daring greatly; the loser – cold, timid, and afraid – dares little.

Based on that definition, then, it's not really the scoreboard that defines why losers lose. In fact, it's worth noting that if some comparison to others is their only measure, then even the loser, ironically, will stumble into winning once in a while. No matter who you are, if you're willing to look hard enough, you can surely find someone out there who's worse than you. Or maybe it's your lucky day, where the ball just happens to bounce your way or you catch that break you've sat around hoping for. Here's the point: it's entirely possible for you to luck into winning, but you can't luck into becoming a winner. You can't accidentally chase excellence. You can't cheat the process of becoming a champion.

That's a choice each of us has to make each day – sometimes many times a day – whether or not we'll step into the arena and chase excellence. It's a choice with life-changing implications. Choosing to be a champion may seem glamorous on the surface, but when you dig deeper you see that it won't earn you less work and more attention. A closer look reveals just the opposite is true. It'll actually earn you *more work* and *less attention*. You'll be dustier and sweatier and maybe even bloodier than before, and dustier, sweatier, and bloodier for sure than those clean, comfortable critics picking you apart from the safe side of the wall. But this decision – to step into the arena and chase excellence – is the first of many winning choices that separates you, the champion, from everyone else.

KEY CONCEPTS FOR
CHASING EXCELLENCE

- Chasing excellence is about more than just winning. It's about the process of becoming the best you can be.

- The successful outcome is where the champion is recognized, but the process, the journey – the pursuit of excellence – that's where the champion is made.

- Excellence can be exhibited anywhere. In fact, whatever you're doing today, and wherever you're doing it, it can be done like a champion.

- A champion is committed to the whole story, not just to the highlights.

- You can luck into winning, but you can't luck into becoming a winner. You can't accidentally chase excellence. You can't cheat the process of becoming a champion.

WHAT CHAMPIONS SAY ABOUT
CHASING EXCELLENCE

"Excellence is to do a common thing in an uncommon way." *-Booker T. Washington*

"The will to win, the desire to succeed, the urge to reach our potential...these are the keys that will unlock the door to personal excellence." *-Confucius*

"It takes time to create excellence. If it could be done quickly, more people would do it." *-John Wooden*

"If you are going to achieve excellence in the big things, you develop the habit in little matters. Excellence is not an exception; it is a prevailing attitude." *-Colin Powell*

"If a man is called to be a street sweeper, he should sweep streets even as Michelangelo painted, or Beethoven composed music or Shakespeare wrote poetry. He should sweep the streets so well that all the hosts of heaven and earth will pause to say, 'Here lived a great street sweeper who did his job well.'" *-Martin Luther King, Jr.*

CHAPTER 2:

CHAMPIONS MAKE WINNING CHOICES

DO WHAT CHAMPIONS DO

Every four years, when voters in our country go to the polls and cast their ballots, they are actively participating in one of the great acts of freedom we possess in the United States. It's the power we've been given to choose. Every vote cast is a choice made, and at the end of the day it's we, the people who decide who'll lead us on the path moving forward. If we don't like the path that's been chosen, then soon enough we'll have the freedom to choose again, this time a new leader and a new path. The power to choose: it's the greatest of individual freedoms we possess.

In many ways, each of us holds an individual election in life each day (and often many times each day) to determine which "us" will govern our lives. Will we elect the best version of ourselves, or settle for someone else? Will we choose the champion or the loser? Unfortunately, human nature encourages us to waltz unwittingly into our personal voting booth, and casually and carelessly select the inferior candidate. Our default, auto-pilot setting points us toward the path of least resistance. Toward the easy, comfortable, convenient choice. It pulls us toward mediocrity. It encourages us to be average.

On the surface, it might appear that champions are wired differently than everyone else, that they've got some unique ability to master that mediocrity. In truth, though, champions feel that same pull we all do. Despite how they feel, however, champions simply choose better than everyone else. They choose intentionally. Mindfully. Exceptionally. By repeatedly making that winning choice – by casting an individual vote for excellence again and again – champions have trained themselves to be great.

It's cliché to say, but it's true: you were not born a winner or a loser; you were born a chooser. In the same way, champions were not born champions. They were built and developed and refined, one winning choice at a time, and it works the same for you. Certainly there are some circumstances in life that have existed outside your control, and some of them may have powerfully impacted the story of your life. But champions recognize that who they are is not the sum total of their circumstances. Who they are is the sum total of their decisions.

The collective power of our choices is a great example of the process at work. Being your best starts with a choice, a single vote you cast in this daily election cycle. Wherever you are and whatever you're doing, will you step into the arena and be your champion self today? This one individual choice is all you can control. But choosing your best self this one time doesn't make you a champion. It's the collection of votes, that sum total of your choices, that determines not what you just did, but who you actually are. Champions are champions not because they've made a single winning choice, but because they've trained themselves to continually make winning choices. Each and every choice – made each and every day – continues to tally the vote count, and with it the proof of their identity as a winner.

The good news is that this democratic election process puts the power in your hands. In a world where it's easy to dwell on all that exists beyond our control, as a champion you see clearly just how many important choices you do get to make. *You* get to decide if you'll take winning action today. *You* decide if you'll value what's really important. *You* decide how much heart goes into your work. *You* decide your level of effort. *You* decide your response to challenge or adversity. *You* decide to seek improvement. *You* decide to get coached. *You* decide how you'll treat others. *You* decide whether you'll go all-in competing to win. *You* decide your attitude. Each one of those choices is critical to your becoming a champion, and no one else gets to make those choices but you.

The bad news about this process is we can only develop or re-develop our identity one vote, one decision at a time. If you've been tallying votes for your mediocre self, then who you are at your best – though it still exists – is probably trailing significantly at the polls. You have the time and the power to resurrect your champion self, but changing your reputation, your identity, and your character can't happen overnight. It can only happen one champion-minded choice at a time. If your history of poor choices makes the magnitude of that comeback feel like moving a mountain, then just focus on what you can control: making the next winning choice you've got in front of you. As the Chinese proverb puts it, "The man who moves a mountain begins by carrying away small stones."

The lure to choose what's easy, what's comfortable, and what's convenient will always exist. As a candidate in this race, your inner loser is constantly running a dirty campaign. His message is filled with lies, with false hope and empty promises about the value of that comfort and convenience. Your mediocre self will quietly but relentlessly be reminding you that if you simply take a look at the lives of those around you, his way – the easy way – is the popular choice. Mediocrity is always running a smear campaign against your champion self. It's not worth all the work, it says. Won't you look foolish, all marred up in that arena by sweat and dust and blood? Play it safe. Keep yourself clean. Steer clear of the arena.

As a champion, denying that temptation to choose mediocrity doesn't get easier…you just get better. You get stronger and smarter. Every time you make the right choice, despite the resistance, you take another step forward in the process of developing winning habits. By intentionally, mindfully, and exceptionally choosing to be a champion in whatever you're facing today, you are disciplining and preparing yourself to make the same choice easier next time. It takes time, discipline, and effort to build a habit, but if you're committed to chasing excellence, you recognize it as necessary work.

The ancient Greek philosopher Aristotle confirmed the importance of habit-building when he said, "We are what we repeatedly do. Excellence, therefore, is not an act, but a habit." When you do the work it takes to make your best self the default, then you are repeatedly, habitually casting votes for the type of person you want to be, and in the process further cementing your identity as a champion.

Champions understand that in this life, we aren't who we want to be. We are instead who we've trained ourselves to be – who we've elected to be, over the course of time with each individual vote we've cast. In the big, defining moments, under the spotlight of the big stage, the loser will be hoping he can rise to the occasion. But the champion knows that, unfortunately in life, we don't rise to the occasion. Instead, as the Navy Seals put it, we perform at the level of our training. You are and will be who your choices have made you. By choosing the way of the champion, you'll be great when it really matters, and when people dig deep to uncover why, they'll see it's because that's who you've prepared yourself to be. It's what you've trained for. It's what you've chosen.

KEY CONCEPTS FOR
MAKING WINNING CHOICES

- You were not born a winner or a loser; you were born a chooser.

- Champions recognize that who they are is not the sum total of their circumstances. Who they are is the sum total of their decisions.

- Each and every choice – made each and every day – continues to build up the vote count, and with it the champion's identity as a winner.

- As a champion, denying that temptation to choose mediocrity doesn't get easier...you just get better. You get stronger and smarter.

- When you do the work it takes to make your best self the default, then you are repeatedly, habitually casting votes for the type of person you want to be, and in the process further cementing your identity as a champion.

WHAT CHAMPIONS SAY ABOUT
MAKING WINNING CHOICES

"Life is a matter of choices, and every choice you make makes you." *-John Maxwell*

"We are the creative voice of our own life, and through our own decisions rather than our conditions, if we carefully learn to do certain things, we can accomplish those goals." *-Steven Covey*

"There is a choice you make in everything you do. So keep in mind that in the end, the choice you make, makes you." *-John Wooden*

"I am who I am today because of the choices I made yesterday." *-Eleanor Roosevelt*

"It is in your moments of decision that your destiny is shaped." *-Tony Robbins*

CHAPTER 3:

CHAMPIONS CULTIVATE THEIR HIDDEN TALENT

DO WHAT CHAMPIONS DO

On the surface, it might appear that champions have something others don't, some unique gift that's opened their door to greatness – a door that remains closed and locked for the rest of us. In some ways this is true. God has not dispersed all His gifts equally. As we stated already, some people in your line of work may have gifts, either physically or mentally, that you don't have. What Michael Jordan was given to use on a basketball court, or what Thomas Edison was given to use in a laboratory, or what Pablo Casals was given to play his cello is different than what you or I were given to use in those areas. Those unique gifts and talents are easy to see. They're an important part of why those people are considered the best, and usually part of why anyone is great at anything, including the things you and I want to be great at, too.

This kind of talent you might call surface-level talent. It's easy to see and point to as justification for why winners win and why others don't. For why some people become champions and why some are forced to settle for something less.

But if you dig deeper into the lives, minds, and experiences of champions in any area, you might find a different reality. Yes, people like Jordan and Edison and Casals were blessed with gifts unique to each of them, and that played an important part in their success. There's no denying that. But I would contend that each of those men – and most of the other champions you'd find in any field – would reject the idea that surface-level talent was the primary factor in their success. It played a role, of course, but there was something else they possessed deep inside that, once recognized and developed, really set them apart. It was their Hidden Talent.

Michael Jordan said himself that his most valuable asset wasn't his shooting, his dribbling, or his vertical leap. It was his coachability. "My best skill was that I was coachable," he said. "I was a sponge and aggressive to learn." While most of the world was glamorizing and glorifying his athleticism, it was his ability to get coached that Jordan believed made him great.

Edison is fondly remembered as America's most masterful inventor, but it was his ability to overcome adversity – the same adversity that led most of the scientific world to deem the invention of the electric light bulb impossible – that defined his legacy. He fell short of his goal again and again, but unlike his competition, he refused to quit. In response to his numerous missteps, he famously proclaimed, "I have not failed 10,000 times – I've successfully found 10,000 ways that will not work." Thomas Edison was a genius in a world of geniuses. It was his perseverance and his resilience that made him unique.

And Casals? He was acclaimed as the world's preeminent cellist and even played for two sitting U.S. presidents. Of course he was immensely gifted as a musician, but learning, growing, and improving was actually his defining talent. Despite his reputation as the best there ever was, Casals continued working on his craft by practicing his instrument into old age. On the day he died, at the age of 96, he had practiced his scales for a number of hours already. A few years earlier, at 93, a friend asked Casals why he continued to practice as diligently as ever. Casals replied, "Because I think I'm making progress." Pablo Casals, on the surface? Elite level cellist. But when you dig deeper, what really set him apart? His elite level commitment to improve.

Jordan's coachability, Edison's resilience, and Casals' desire for improvement are all examples of Hidden Talent. Like any talent, each one is an innate gift that, once recognized and developed, separates its owner from everyone else. Hidden Talents are the traits, attributes, and behaviors that champions have sown into their being. They're the behaviors champions develop that make them champions. When you work to uncover what really makes a champion a champion — in sports or music, in art or business, in relationships or in life — you find these unique qualities:

HIDDEN TALENT

• LOVING THE GAME
• OVERCOMING ADVERSITY
• GETTING COACHED
• TAKING RISKS
• GIVING YOUR BEST
• SEEKING IMPROVEMENT
• BEING A TEAMMATE
• CHOOSING A POSITIVE ATTITUDE

This kind of talent we've called hidden for good reason. It can be hard to quantify. Surface-level talent is usually tangible. You can measure Michael Jordan's vertical leap, or Thomas Edison's IQ, or Casals' perfect tone quality. The stats prove their value and their preeminence. But it's hard to put a measurement on someone's coachability or their resilience or their desire to improve.

Hidden Talents are the *intangibles* – qualities that can be hard to define with stats or numbers. Even though it's clear that champions just seem to have "that thing" or just "get it" in a way that most others don't, it's not always easy to point a finger directly at what that thing is or what it is exactly that they get. Hidden Talent can be hard to measure, but if you really dig deep into a winner's character and mindset, you usually find it in abundance.

Another reason these talents are hidden is because in this day and age, we're easily seduced by what we see on the surface. Michael Jordan hitting the game-winner and hoisting another championship trophy is way more glamorous than Michael Jordan, humbly and intently listening and looking for advice from his coach on how he could do better. The headline in his bio reads, "Edison's genius changed the world!" not "Edison failed way more than he succeeded, but was tough enough to handle it anyway." And while history celebrates Casals playing under the spotlight at Carnegie Hall, there's not much acclaim for all those nights he spent alone in the dark, practicing 'til his fingers bled.

Surface-level talent is loud. It's alluring. It's fun. Whether or not it's the reason why those who've won have actually won, unfortunately today, is a secondary issue. But while the talent we see on the surface is mostly style, Hidden Talent is all substance. It's the boring, simple, infallible foundation of excellence. It's not a SportsCenter highlight or a front-page headline. It's often a humble, quiet footnote, working away silently and superbly outside the spotlight without any attention or fanfare. It's overlooked and underappreciated amidst a lot of noise and nonsense. But the truth is, when you strip all the flashy stuff away, what you find hidden underneath is what makes a champion a champion.

Sadly, these talents are hidden too because, deep down, many of us don't want to expose the truth these talents present: that is, that each one of them is available to each one of us. This of course should be news worth celebrating, especially if we're really serious about becoming our best. But bringing this truth to light – that in many ways you and I could have what Jordan and Edison and Casals had, and exactly what we need to be champions ourselves – also tears down many of the loser's excuses and explanations.

Losers want to believe that they just don't have what it takes. That's exactly what the loser in you wants you to believe. But the truth is, in whatever area you're competing today, at some point someone with less surface-level talent than you has probably achieved more than you. Someone with less natural, surface-level ability than you has already done something you may be thinking you can't accomplish. Why? Because they've stepped into the arena and you haven't. Because they've made winning choices and you haven't. Because they've recognized and developed their Hidden Talent, and you haven't.

When you dig deep, the differences between champions and losers become strikingly clear. It's all about their Hidden Talent. Champions love it while losers suffer through it. Champions give their best; losers go through the motions. Champions are tough, hungry, and humble. Losers are soft, smug, and easily satisfied. Champions win by bringing out the best in those around them; losers are threatened or annoyed by others. Champions take risks while losers play it safe. Champions choose a positive, productive attitude. Losers settle for something less.

Here's the good news. Whoever you are, whatever you've done prior to this very moment, and in whatever areas you believe you are or aren't unique, special, or talented…you have been gifted in these important areas. Cultivating your talent, and turning these gifts into reality, is a long process. That process starts with "Recognition" – that's really what this book provides, a chance to recognize and uncover the gifts you've been given. This is the important first step in the process. Then comes "Development" – the hard work it takes to turn your potential into reality. Development is the long, difficult journey towards your very best. Finally comes "Separation" – using who you've become to separate yourself from the competition. That's the fun third step.

Embracing this process and the work that comes with it can lead you to new levels of success. But more importantly, it can move you closer to what's really worth chasing – excellence. Can you create a vision of that version of yourself, fully developed in these most important areas? You, loving the work and giving your best. You, tough, hungry, and humble. You, bringing out the best in those around you.

You, courageously taking risks. You, with a positive, productive attitude.

That's a vision of you, in the arena. It's you at your best. It's you, the champion.

KEY CONCEPTS FOR
CULTIVATING YOUR
HIDDEN TALENT

- Champions in any area possess something deep inside that, once recognized and developed, really sets them apart. You might call it their Hidden Talent.

- Hidden Talents are the traits, attributes, and behaviors that champions have sown into their being.

- While some talents are tangible and measurable, Hidden Talents are *intangibles* – qualities that can be harder to measure or make out.

- In this day and age, we are easily seduced by what we see on the surface.

- While the talent we see on the surface is mostly style, Hidden Talent is all substance. It's the boring, simple, infallible foundation of excellence.

WHAT CHAMPIONS SAY ABOUT
CULTIVATING YOUR
HIDDEN TALENT

<u>Loving the Game</u>
"Success is no accident. It is hard work, perseverance, learning, studying, sacrifice, and most of all, love of what you are doing or learning to do." *-Pele*

<u>Giving Your Best</u>
"To give anything less than your best is to sacrifice the gift." *-Steve Prefontaine*

<u>Overcoming Adversity</u>
"I think a champion is defined not by their wins, but by how they recover when they fall."
-Serena Williams

<u>Seeking Improvement</u>
"The principle is competing against yourself. It's all about self-improvement, about being better than you were the day before." *-Steve Young*

<u>Getting Coached</u>
"If I'm not doing it right, I want coach to tell me so I can fix it." *-Steph Curry*

WHAT CHAMPIONS SAY ABOUT
CULTIVATING YOUR
HIDDEN TALENT

Being a Teammate
"I am a member of a team, and I rely on the team,
I defer to it and sacrifice for it, because the team,
not the individual, is the ultimate champion."
-*Mia Hamm*

Taking Risks
"He who is not courageous enough to take risks
will accomplish nothing in life." -*Muhammad Ali*

Choosing a Positive Attitude
"Virtually nothing is impossible in this world if you
just put your mind to it and maintain a positive
attitude." -*Lou Holtz*

THERE'S MORE TO THE
CHAMPION THAN WHAT
YOU SEE ON THE SURFACE.

CHAPTER 4:

RECOGNITION

THE IMPORTANT FIRST STEP

Before any of us can ever tap into the gifts we've been given, we first have to recognize those gifts. If you've been given a gift, but don't recognize its existence, then does it really exist? Is a gift, either unacknowledged or unreceived, really a gift at all?

Let's pretend for your next birthday I get you a present. I wrap it up nicely, put your name on the tag, and bring it to your home. But, instead of handing it to you or setting it out where you can see it, I hide it under your bed and never mention it again. What value would that gift have?

What if I get you a present, bring it to your home and set it right in front of you, but purposely or not, you refuse to acknowledge it? "Ahem…I got you something," I finally say. "This is for you." Still you refuse to recognize it for what it is. "No it isn't," you reply. Despite my continuing efforts, you refuse to acknowledge what it is you've been given. We both move on with life, but the gift remains – unacknowledged and unopened – gathering dust there forever.

If a gift isn't recognized as a gift, then it isn't really a gift. It's only a gift once it's recognized, acknowledged, and accepted by the one it was meant for. Our talent can be described the same way. We can be given any number of gifts, but if we don't recognize and receive them, then they may as well not exist at all.

For any talented person, recognizing their gift was the first step in cultivating their talent. What if, purposely or not, Michael Jordan just never recognized what he was capable of with a basketball, and instead spent his life toiling away as a mediocre musician? What if, despite his musical talent, Pablo Casals blindly decided to devote his time and energy to basketball instead of to cello? The gifts they'd been given in their area of excellence, if overlooked or ignored, may as well not have existed at all. The same is true for each of us, in any area where we're uniquely talented. We cannot develop a gift until we recognize its existence.

This is step one in the process. At some point, either on their own or with some help, anyone who cultivates a talent first recognizes that talent. Sometimes they stumble upon it themselves; sometimes others point it out. Usually it's some combination of both. Jordan, Edison, and Casals each had prominent people in their lives who helped them identify the talent they possessed, someone who said, "Hey! With some time and effort, you could be really good at this stuff! You should do this more." That's one of the important purposes of this book – to help you see, with more clarity than ever before or maybe for the first time altogether, some of the gifts you've been given. This is me saying, "Hey! With some time and effort, you could be really good at this stuff! You should do this more." Of course, what you decide to do from here is up to you.

Recognition is an important step, but it is, of course, only the first step – and also the easiest step, I might add – in bringing your talent to life. At this point, you could replace the word "gift" with the word "potential." That's really all we're talking about here. What's possible, as opposed to what's actual. Not what is, but what could be. Potential is an interesting word because its value changes based on where you stand. If you're standing before your potential, then "what could be" feels pretty promising. But if you're standing beyond your potential, then the idea of "what could've been" can feel pretty painful. Few words have the power to offer both as much promise, or as much pain, as that word potential.

Here's the promising prospect of potential. Once you recognize a gift or talent, the idea of who you can become gains clarity. A vision for what's possible can get you excited, and maybe get those around you – those who've also recognized your gift – excited, too. For those who take that potential and develop it, there's a lot to look forward to. They recognize that with a lot of hard work, turning this gift into reality can make them better than they were before, and better than many of those they'll be competing with and against moving forward. It can make them special. Unique. Set apart. That's fun to think about.

But, unfortunately, potential can be painful, too. For many people, what's possible never becomes what's actual. What they're capable of doing, achieving, or becoming far exceeds what they actually do or achieve or become. Recognizing that you've been given a gift is only great if it's followed by a series of winning choices. Until then, it's worthless.

If you choose poorly, your potential goes untapped and your gift unopened. Sadly, instead of becoming special, unique, or set apart – someone who did the work, developed the gift, and separated themselves – you join the long list of those who could've, or would've, or should've. Who could've accomplished more. Who would've really been something special. Who, regretfully, should've taken the gift they were given and brought it to life.

Recognizing Your Hidden Talent

So step one, in the process of turning your Hidden Talent from potential to reality, is simply recognizing the gifts you've been given. You have the ability to love what you do. To give your very best. To overcome adversity, and to seek improvement. *You can* get coached, be a teammate, and take risks. And you can do it all with a positive attitude.

Maybe right now you're thinking, "Okay, hang on. How are these talents? Isn't talent only given to a select few? I've got them, great…but so does everyone else!" That's a fair enough point, and if that's enough for you to bail on this idea, so be it. But here's the counterpoint: who cares? Who cares who's been given the gift? That number – the number of people who've been gifted in a certain area – is *way* less important than what those who've been gifted *choose to do with it.*

Remember, only those who recognize their gifts, and then, more importantly, choose to develop those gifts become special, unique, or set apart. Just because someone (or everyone, for that matter) *can* doesn't mean they *will.* In fact, look around and validate that reality in every Hidden Talent area. Everyone *can* love the game, but who actually does? Everyone *can* give their best, but who actually does? It's only important to acknowledge that everyone's been gifted in these areas because it verifies that *you've* been gifted here. When it comes to overcoming adversity or seeking improvement or taking risks – or any other Hidden Talent area – it's not most important to see that everyone has this potential. It's most important to see that *you* do.

No matter how much you might want to jump like Jordan, invent like Edison, or play like Casals, it probably just isn't in the cards. You probably haven't been given those gifts. That's important to see, because the more time you spend wishing you'd been given something you weren't, trying to fake like you have something you don't, or envying what someone else has that you haven't, the less time you spend recognizing, appreciating, and developing what you *have* been given. And since you can't control what haven't been given, there's no use dwelling on it.

Champions control the controllables, and the truth is, you can be a champion because you have the potential to do all the things champions do. When you define it that way, it's clear that developing what it takes to become a champion is actually a choice – your choice. So recognize what you do have, make the winning choice to go all in on maximizing the gifts you've been given, and use them to become the best you possible. If you do, success is bound to follow.

There is one last bit of recognition, when it comes to your Hidden Talent, that's worth emphasizing, and that's simply recognizing that you cannot be your best without it.

Take a minute to compare, in each of the Hidden Talent areas, you with vs. you without. If you're serious about becoming your best – in any area of life – your Hidden Talent is required. Compare you, who's developed the ability to give your very best vs. you who hasn't. Or you, who's genuinely committed to seeking improvement vs. you who's not. Who's winning that match-up? It's really not rocket science. You have to recognize that just as Hidden Talent is and has been the primary difference-maker in the lives of so many great people – athletes, inventors musicians, and more – your Hidden Talent is *the* primary difference-maker in determining who you become. And in these areas, you have limitless potential.

Recognizing your gifts and what they can do for you is easy. But simply acknowledging your potential doesn't turn it into reality. After all, if everyone *can* do all these things, then why would anyone – especially someone who's recognized the importance of their own effort or toughness or ability to work with others, for instance – settle for anything less? When it's clear that anyone could choose to do what a champion does, then why doesn't everyone do it? Because potential, as we've emphasized already, is merely what's possible, not what's actual. It takes more than potential to be great. Your talent, promising though it might be, is worthless until it's developed.

That next step, development – turning potential into reality – is really where it's at. Where the work's at. Where the struggle's at. Where the growth's at. Then and only then, when we move beyond simply recognizing our gifts and get busy doing the work it takes to develop them, can any of us do more than just hope we rise to the important occasions in life.

Recognition helps us see what's possible, but when we choose to intentionally and mindfully step into the arena of development each day, then we actually begin the journey towards our very best.

KEY CONCEPTS FOR
RECOGNITION

- We can be given any number of gifts, but if we don't recognize and receive them, then they may as well not exist at all.

- Recognizing that you've been given a gift is only great if it's followed by a series of winning choices. Until then, it's worthless.

- The number of people who've been given a gift in a certain area is way less important than what those who've been gifted *choose to do with it.*

- When it comes to any Hidden Talent area, it's not most important to see that everyone has this potential. It's most important to see that *you* do.

- Just as Hidden Talent is and has been the primary difference-maker in the lives of so many great people - athletes, inventors, musicians, and more - your Hidden Talent is the primary difference-maker in determining who you become.

WHAT CHAMPIONS SAY ABOUT
RECOGNITION

"Nothing is more common than unsuccessful men with talent." *-Calvin Coolidge*

"It's not what you got, it's what you use that makes a difference." *-Zig Ziglar*

"If we did all the things we were capable of, we would literally astound ourselves." *-Thomas Edison*

"A lot of guys have potential written on their tombstones." *-Kevin McHale*

"The only person you are destined to become is the person you decide to be." *-Ralph Waldo Emerson*

CHAPTER 5:

DEVELOPMENT

THE DIFFICULT SECOND STEP

If recognizing our gifts is the easy first step in becoming a champion, then developing them is the long, slow journey that follows. Recognition requires thought and reflection; many people are willing to pay that price. Development, on the other hand, requires work. And work. And more work. That's a heftier price, one fewer are willing to pay. Like the man in the arena Roosevelt described, development requires the doing of deeds. It requires some dust, some sweat, maybe even some blood. For many, simply recognizing their gift and living in that potential is enough. But for the champion, the work has just begun. Forget just recognizing potential. The champion is committed to realizing it.

Remember that gift I'm planning to get you for your next birthday? Let's say I set it right out there in the open for you. You walk in on your big day and see it sitting there, draped with a big bow and your name on the tag. "Thanks for the gift!" you exclaim. You clearly recognize it exists and that it's meant for you. "Well, open it!" I say. "No," you reply, "I'm good. I really appreciate the thought, though." And then, you leave it there. Day after day, week after week it sits, untouched.

You tell guests about the nice gift you've been given and how thankful you are to have gotten it, but it remains unopened and unused.

You clearly identified that you'd been given a gift. But if you left it there collecting dust, what good was it? If you never unpacked it, never uncovered what it was, and never put it to use, I'm not sure you could still call it a gift. Gifts aren't meant just to be recognized; they're meant to be utilized.

Look at Jordan or Edison or Casals again. Each of them was given a unique gift – Jordan as an athlete, Edison as an inventor, Casals as a musician. They were fortunate to have been given these gifts and equally fortunate to have recognized them. But then what happened? Did each champion kick back, relax, and enjoy the benefits of their talent from then on? Of course not! Despite some sort of delusional fantasy our culture has created about the way talent works – a fantasy many of us have bought into ourselves – that's not reality for anyone. That's just the easy first step. Those people became who they became not because they recognized their gift, but because they developed it.

Too often when people think of excellence in any area, the image that naively comes to mind is of that surface-level talent. Jordan effortlessly swishing the step-back game-winner at the buzzer. The cheers raining down on Edison as he flips the switch and illuminates the world. Casals masterfully manipulating bow on string, and making musical magic. But in reality, most of the images that accurately depict the champion's experience in the arena are not nearly so glamorous.

The humble reality of excellence is much less flattering. It's Michael Jordan, alone in a gym hours after everyone else has left. He's not working on his step-back jumper until he gets it right; he's working until he can't get it wrong. It's Edison, a year and a half into his long, slow journey to the light bulb's creation, sitting alone in his office at the dusk of another long day. He's flipping through notebooks and looseleafs, some of the 40,000 pages of notes he's taken on this journey. It's this gifted man, striving valiantly to solve what many thought was an unsolvable mystery, coming up short again and again on his way to achievement. The humble reality is Casals – the best – working again today on the basics. Unlike most of us, he understands that excellence is built on the foundation of fundamentals.

The same can be said for the champions living, working, and winning wherever you are. Forget the legends and history makers known to the world. Who is the standard-bearer of talent in your field, in *your* world? Who's the one in the winner's circle, hoisting the trophy, and making the headlines where you are? The one who strikes you as not just successful, but excellent? If you're an athlete, maybe it's the best player in your conference or division. If you're a businessman, it could be the person regularly recognized for exemplary work in your company or your competitor's. Whoever it is, it may be easy to resentfully envision that person having all those things you wish you had – the recognition, the glory, the success – and having them effortlessly and easily.

It's time to stop envisioning that naïve picture of success and recognize instead that perhaps those champion people have done – in this most humble, most unflattering, but most important area of talent development – what you haven't. It's possible, of course, that you could be doing just as much development work as they are, and they're simply farther along in the process than you. But maybe it's time for you to see that they aren't actually more talented than you. Maybe they aren't just lucky. Maybe they've simply done more with their gifts than you've done with yours. Maybe – gulp – they've done *more* with *less* than what you have.

This is perhaps the biggest reason so many people die with the word "potential" written on their tombstones, because it's easier to blame fate, luck, or lottery for our situation than to accept the hard truth. The hard truth is, champions don't become champions by accident. When we see talented people, we usually see them well into the development phase, and when someone makes something awesome look easy – like Jordan or Edison or Casals, or that person you've been picturing doing excellent stuff in your world – it's easy to acclaim their gift without acclaiming their work. We fool ourselves into thinking it should be easy. We say things like, "Man, that person at the top has a gift. He is so talented."

But the person on top of the mountain didn't fall there. Now, again, not anyone can do anything. But more than we'd like to admit, the man on top of the mountain has spent a little bit of his time recognizing the gift he's been given, and the majority of his time working to maximize that gift. He's spent a little time recognizing that he could climb the mountain, then most of his time *doing the work* it takes to climb it.

Out of the spotlight and the headlines, the champion's been working, trying, struggling, learning, and improving. It's way more than the gift that makes a champion a champion. It's that climb – the countless hours spent mastering their craft, honing their skill, and refining their talent on the side of the mountain, not at the top – that turns what could potentially be into what actually is. In any area where you've been gifted, the same will be true for you.

Developing Your Hidden Talent

Turning your Hidden Talent from potential into reality, from what could possibly be into what actually is, requires the same process. It's at least as easy, and maybe even easier, to overlook or diminish the reality of this process in these areas as it is any other. If everyone has been given these gifts – if everyone has the potential to be great in these areas – then why do some people have it and some people don't?

Why can some people love the game and some can't?
Why can some people give their best and some can't?
Why can some people overcome adversity and some can't?
Why can some people seek improvement and some can't?
Why can some people get coached and some can't?
Why can some people be a teammate and some can't?
Why can some people take risks and some can't?
Why can some people choose a positive attitude and some can't?

Are these abilities determined simply by luck? Have these people won some sort of intangibles lottery? Have they, by some magic stroke of fortune, acquired these skills so crucial to success in the world while the rest of us simply didn't? Fortunately, the answer is no. The person on top of each of these mountains didn't fall there. Like with any talent, they started by recognizing that they've been given a unique gift, a potentially difference-making ability. Then, more importantly, they've done the hard work it takes to turn a potentially difference-making ability into a difference-making reality.

So what does the process of developing your Hidden Talent look like? As with all talent development, it starts with a winning choice. In any one of those areas, the process starts with a simple decision to act. Development cannot and will not begin until you choose to step into the arena. Someone in your life – a parent, or a coach, a boss or mentor, or some author writing to you in a book – can help you recognize that your effort, or your toughness, or your courage, or any other Hidden Talent can set you apart. Someone can explain to you how important these attributes are. You can observe someone else live them out and demonstrate them for you, and you can know all the answers when someone asks you about the choices you should make. But no one else can step into the arena but you. No one can give you what a champion's got – you have to decide to experience it and develop it and create it on your own. You have to *earn it* for yourself.

Earning it starts with a willingness to say, "I don't just recognize that I'm capable of _____. (Fill in the blank with any Hidden Talent area.) I'm going to do it." What will happen when you decide to do it, to step into the arena? Early in the process, who knows? As Roosevelt said, you may succeed triumphantly or you may fail miserably. But by choosing to act, you take a step forward, and in doing so you start learning, growing, and improving for yourself.

If it does go well, great. Of course, one choice made is better than nothing, but don't forget that one choice doesn't define your character or create your identity. It's simply one vote you've cast for your champion self. Choosing to overcome a challenge one time makes you tougher, but it does not make you tough. The same goes for an individual choice you make to show your passion, to give your best, or to get better. To get coached or to be a great teammate. To take a risk or to choose a positive attitude. One choice makes it something you did, not someone you are. That's the goal of development, of course – to make each of these Hidden Talents more than a single act, but instead a consistent habit and part of your character and identity. One choice doesn't get you there, but it does allow you to uncover and clarify for yourself the reality, in that moment of chasing excellence, of how it feels to live like a champion.

Recognizing that you *can* do it, and then choosing *to try* to do it, and then *actually doing it* is important because it gives you something that's so important for this long, difficult journey. It gives you pride. It's that feeling – not just a concept in your mind, but a feeling deep in your heart – that says, "I did it." That pride you feel when you step into the arena, and WIN – especially if you've not experienced it before – is an awesome, unique, empowering feeling. No one else can give you that kind of pride; it's something you can only create for yourself, which is probably why it feels so good. The pride that comes with success serves as fuel for the long, difficult journey that development requires. It invigorates your spirit and inspires you to choose well again.

On the other hand, recognizing that you *can* do it, and then choosing *to try* to do it, and then *failing to do it* can also be helpful. It gives you a different kind of fuel: regret. It's that feeling in your heart that says, "I could have done that. I should have…and I didn't." The regret you feel when you try and fail in an area that you've recognized as important – that feeling stinks. It stinks, but it's valuable, because now you're recognizing that you can do better. You should do better. You *have to* do better. If you're a competitor, this is the kind of thought that eats you up inside. It motivates your spirit and inspires you to get in there and try again.

Like anything in life, the more you experience this development – the more practice you get – the more refined you become. Every time you step back in the arena and try again, you improve. One winning choice becomes two. Two becomes four, and four becomes eight. Over time, fueled by both the pride of your past success and the regret of your previous failure, your champion-minded decisions gradually become champion-minded habits. Now you're electing regularly to think, act, and live like a champion. You're elevating the level of your training, you're re-creating a new, better identity, and you're becoming your most talented self.

It's at this point you'll probably realize two things. First, you realize that this process takes even longer than you imagined. In fact, you may come to realize that there really is no finish line on this journey of developing your Hidden

Talent. Every day is a new opportunity to refine your gifts, cultivate your talent, and validate your identity as a champion. Even the most menial tasks are suddenly opportunities for you to prove again to yourself exactly who you are.

Secondly, you realize that you are more prepared, more excited, and more determined than ever to step into the arena. Your opponents in today's game – others standing between you and success, or the mediocre self standing between you and excellence – hasn't gotten any weaker or less wily. But you're stronger, smarter, and better than you've ever been…and best of all, you're still developing.

KEY CONCEPTS FOR
DEVELOPMENT

- When we see talented people, we usually see them well into the development phase, and when someone makes something awesome look easy, it's easy to acclaim their gift without acclaiming their work.

- Out of the spotlight and the headlines, the champion's been working, trying, struggling, learning, and improving.

- It's way more than the gift that makes a champion a champion. It's that climb – the countless hours spent mastering their craft, honing their skill, and refining their talent on the side of the mountain, not at the top – that turns what could potentially be into what actually is.

- No one else can step into the arena but you, and no one else can give you what a champion's got. You have to *earn it* for yourself.

- Every day is a new opportunity to refine your gifts, cultivate your talent, and validate your identity as a champion.

WHAT CHAMPIONS SAY ABOUT
DEVELOPMENT

"Champions don't become champions when they win an event, but in the hours, weeks, months, and years they spend preparing for it." *-Michael Jordan*

"Becoming your best is an on-going process." *-Mike Krzyzewski*

"Shallow men believe in luck. Strong men believe in cause and effect." *-Ralph Waldo Emerson*

"Success is a result of consistent practice of winning skills and actions. There is nothing miraculous about the process. There is no luck involved." *-Bill Russell*

"Today's society wants to skip the process, and I hate that." *-Tom Izzo*

CHAPTER 6:

SEPARATION

THE FUN THIRD STEP

If recognition is the important first step, and development is the difficult next step, then separation is the fun final step. It's the reward you get for the hard work you've done, for turning your gift from potential into reality. By doing the work, you've separated yourself – not only from those around you, but also from the person you used to be. You are unique, uncommon, set apart. And now, at this stage of the game, you get to enjoy the benefits that come with it.

Separation is what people see and celebrate. Michael Jordan, Thomas Edison, and Pablo Casals all recognized the talent they'd been given. In the recognition stage, very few noticed and even fewer cared. Then they worked like crazy to develop that talent. Again, in development, it was mostly crickets. But then, as they slowly started to separate themselves, they began to stand out. That's when people took notice.

Suddenly, they were special. Elite. People saw and celebrated the result of their work, and, as is often the case in identifying talented people, generally ignored or overlooked the process it took to get there. When we allow ourselves to do that – ignore or overlook the process – we also ignore or overlook maybe the most important truth tied to our talent: that we can't get to separation until we go through development. We can't get the reward without doing the work. Once again we see, we can't cheat the process.

Like in any area of life, we rarely get what we want or what we hope for. More often, we get what we earn. Therefore if development is the sowing process, that makes separation the reaping. The level at which you work to develop your gifts determines the separation you create. If you work a little to develop your gifts, then you will separate yourself a little. If you work a lot, you will separate yourself a lot. You get out what you put in. You reap what you sow.

Earlier we mentioned that one realization you might come to during the Development phase is that there is no finish line on the journey to developing your talent. That reality may have led you to another, more sobering moment of clarity about the reality of this work. "You mean, to be a champion," you may have asked yourself, "I can *never* stop working, trying, struggling, learning, and improving? I have to keep developing…*forever*?" Yep, that's the choice you make if you're serious about becoming your best in any important area. And let's be honest, that can feel intimidating. It's the sobering truth about life as a champion: the work never ends.

But now that we're here in the Separation phase, I hope you can come to a new, different, more inspiring realization about life as a champion. No, there is no finish line on the journey of developing your talent. But because separation is the by-product of development, that also means that there is no limit to the separation you can create, either. "You mean, to be a champion," I hope you're now realizing, "I can *always* keep getting better, widening the gap, making myself more unique, more uncommon, and more set apart? I get to keep separating myself...*forever?*" That's some encouraging truth about life as a champion: the benefit never ends.

Separating Yourself with Your Hidden Talent

Here we are, finally, at the heart of this book. This idea, how you separate yourself with your Hidden Talent, is really what we've been working to track down. Don't get me wrong, champions are defined partly by their ability to recognize the gifts they've been given, and defined even more by their commitment to the work it takes to develop those gifts. And, as we've emphasized already, you can't cheat that process. But at the heart of it, when it comes to uncovering what makes a champion a champion, this is it.

Champions have done the work it takes to separate themselves from everyone else. They are unique, uncommon, and set apart in many ways – most of all in these areas of Hidden Talent. They are great in these areas that are unrivaled in importance, and yet undeveloped in so many people. Hopefully it's clearer (from the pages you've read through already, and even more so in the pages to come) not just that champions are different, but why.

Here is the separation, in its simplest terms, that champions have created:

Champions love the game; losers endure it.
Champions give their best; losers give something less.

Champions overcome adversity; losers crumble.

Champions seek improvement; losers settle for sufficient.

Champions get coached; losers get defensive.

Champions are teammates; losers are selfish.

Champions take risks; losers take the safe route.

Champions choose a positive attitude; losers choose something less.

It's important for you to recognize the scope of the impact these talents can have. Of course, any talent developed makes its developer unique, and while usually our talent only creates distance in one specific area of life, Hidden Talent helps move you toward your very best in *every area* of life. So the question isn't, "Where does Hidden Talent separate you?" The question is, "Where doesn't it?" In whatever area you're hoping to separate yourself – as an athlete, an inventor, or a musician. In your home or at work, alone or with others – your Hidden Talent creates space.

As you develop this talent, you separate yourself from those around you. And even though the pursuit of success – based on some sort of comparison with others – isn't what drives the champion, it is an important part of the competitive world we live in. In many important areas of life, a crowd of other people will be after the same things you're after – a position, an award, or a title, for instance. By recognizing and then developing your Hidden Talent, you stand out from the crowd and help yourself find success.

If you're an athlete, maybe your goal is to make the team or earn a scholarship, or maybe you want to improve the role you have on the team you're already on – to earn a bigger and better opportunity. You won't be alone in any of those pursuits. Plenty of other competitors are creating goals and honing their skills. So when it's time for the coach to make these important decisions, what is it that makes you stand out? Will your measurables be enough, or is there more that defines who you are and the value you bring?

A coach has many difficult decisions to make – about who makes the team, about who plays where, how much, and in what role, but many of those decisions gain clarity when he or she digs deeper into the character and identity of the team members. On the surface, two competitors may look very similar in terms of their physical skills or athletic talent (their measurables), but competition has a way of exposing what they're really made of on the inside. Their passion for the game. Their effort. Their response to challenge and adversity. Their desire to get better. Their willingness to listen and learn. The way they treat others. Their courage. Their attitude. When what's on the inside gets exposed, then for a coach, clarifying who gives the team the best chance to win and who deserves the opportunity gets significantly easier.

If you're a professional, the last two paragraphs could probably be re-written, in eerily similar fashion, with your pursuit of success in mind. You also won't be alone in your pursuits. Plenty of other competitors are creating goals and honing their skills. So when it's time for the boss to make these important decisions – about who gets hired, or who gets the big account, or who gets the promotion – what is it that makes you stand out? Will your measurables be enough, or is there more that defines who you are and the value you bring? Like a coach, a boss's difficult decisions gain clarity when he or she digs deeper into the character and identity of those jockeying for a new or better position. On the surface, two applicants may look very similar in terms of their measurables (like their sales numbers or performance ratings, for instance), but competition has a way of exposing what they're really made of on the inside. Their passion for the job. Their effort. Their response to challenge and adversity. Their desire to get better. Their willingness to listen and learn. The way they treat others. Their courage. Their attitude. When what's on the inside gets exposed, then for a boss, clarifying who deserves to get the job or the account or the promotion gets significantly easier.

Your Hidden Talent, once developed, separates you from those you'll be competing with and against for life. It helps you stand out in your pursuit of success. But please don't forget that for a champion, success is a pit-stop on a more important journey. As a champion, you are chasing excellence, striving valiantly to reach your full potential and become the very best you can be.

If you're committed to focusing on some sort of comparison, then focus on the only one that really matters: the comparison between who you are and who you used to be. It's the gap you're creating between this current you and the old you. If you're serious about developing your Hidden Talent and becoming the best version of yourself, then this is your most important separation.

Again, here in this pursuit of excellence, there's no place in your life unaffected by the separation your Hidden Talent creates. As an athlete, a student, a professional. As a spouse, a parent, a child, or a sibling. At home, at work, at school. When you're pursuing excellence, your Hidden Talent continually widens the gap between who you used to be and who you're working to become.

It's you, more passionate than ever.
You, more relentless than ever.
You, more resilient than ever.
You, more committed to getting better than ever.
You, more humble and more coachable than ever.
You, more courageous than ever.
You, more positive and more purposeful than ever.

In the following chapters, we'll dig deeper into each Hidden Talent area and uncover what Recognition, Development, and Separation looks like for each. In Recognition, we'll examine the important role each talent plays in helping you become your best. In Development, we'll discuss what it looks like to step into the arena, to compete, and to improve in these areas each day. And in Separation, we'll clarify how, once you commit to that process of improvement, your Hidden Talent continually sets you apart. I hope uncovering what makes a champion a champion in the following pages encourages you to accept the challenge of becoming one for yourself.

KEY CONCEPTS FOR
SEPARATION

- Separation is the reward you get for the hard work you've done, for turning your gift from potential into reality. Separation is what people see and what they celebrate.

- We rarely get what we want or what we hope for. More often, we get what we earn.

- The level at which you work to develop your gifts determines the separation you create. If you work a little to develop your gifts, you will separate yourself a little. If you work a lot, you will separate yourself a lot.

- Any talent developed makes its developer unique, and while usually our talent only creates distance in one specific area of life, Hidden Talent helps move you toward your very best in every area of life.

- If you're committed to focusing on some sort of comparison, then focus on the only one that really matters: the comparison between who you are and who you used to be.

WHAT CHAMPIONS SAY ABOUT
SEPARATION

"The highest reward for a person's toil is not what they get for it, but what they become by it."
-John Ruskin

"The one thing that separates winners from losers is, winners take action." *-Tony Robbins*

"You only get out of it what you put into it."
-Greg Norman

"I am not as good as I ought to be. I am not as good as I want to be. I am not as good as I'm going to be. But I am thankful that I am better than I used to be." *-John Wooden*

"There is no finish line." *-Nike*

CHAPTER 7:

LOVING THE GAME

YOUR HIDDEN TALENT

Loving the Game – Recognition

Every Hidden Talent on our list is important, but there's a reason we're starting here, with Loving the Game. As we've emphasized already, becoming a champion is tough. It will require all you've got – your mind, body, and spirit. Most importantly, it will require your heart. There's a long road ahead of you, and it's your heart that will sustain you along the journey. You need to recognize that your passion and commitment serve as fuel for the hard work to come. As usual, when you put your heart into it, anything's possible.

When most people think of love, it's a feeling that immediately comes to mind. If you've ever fallen in love, then you've probably experienced for yourself the power of your feelings. Love definitely taps into your emotions. Your heart races, your stomach turns, and your palms sweat just from being near that special someone. Love can make you feel all tingly inside.

Feelings are good, and they can be powerful. If we're fortunate, we'll find someone in life who never stops igniting that flame of passion inside us. But the feeling that comes with love isn't constant – it ebbs and flows for everyone. It can ignite a relationship in the short-term, but it's not enough to sustain a relationship over the long haul, when feelings start to fade. Long-term success in any relationship requires more than a feeling; it also requires a commitment. A promise. A pledge.

Married couples who experience long-term relational success haven't floated through life on their feelings. They've more likely faced the same struggle in building and developing a strong marriage that comes with building and developing anything great over time, in any area of life. Sure that feeling may have ruled the relationship at some point, but no one stays all tingly forever. If feelings were all that held a strong partnership together, then no couple would make it. In a relationship that lasts, it's the choices we make – to intentionally commit to and sacrifice for that other person, long after the feeling has faded – that dig their roots in and cultivate a deeper, stronger kind of love that can stand the test of time.

So is that passionate feeling an important part of loving anyone, or anything, in life? Absolutely. You can't be your best at something if you don't feel passionately about it, so we should all be tapping into those feelings. That's easy to see on the surface. But when we dig deeper into what it looks like to develop a stronger love over the long haul, we recognize that feelings alone can't sustain us. There's got to be something more – a deeper level of commitment and sacrifice that we've chosen *regardless of how we feel*, especially if we're hoping to cultivate something that lasts.

Your love for the game must be cultivated the same way. The longer you play and work and do all that's required to pursue excellence in your area, the easier it can be for your flame of passion to fade. Time and fatigue and familiarity – routine, you might call it – can slowly and gradually wear on that flame until, maybe without even really noticing, it barely exists at all anymore. That's why it's important to remember why you started doing this work in the first place.

Why is it that you started playing this game and doing this work? Probably because you really, genuinely loved it. Like a heart racing, stomach turning, palms sweating kind of love. As with any relationship, that feeling comes and goes. It's probably faded some with time and fatigue and familiarity. But remembering why you started in the first place helps you re-connect with that flame, keeps it burning today and sustains it for tomorrow. Be intentional about working to keep that passion alive.

At the same time, recognize that while feelings come and go, an authentic commitment to what you love never does. Love is about our feelings, yes, but it's also about our actions and our choices. Becoming your best is a long, slow, sometimes painful process that requires a massive investment, and it's your love for the game – not just some fleeting feeling inside, but the deeper level commitment and sacrifice you've chosen to make, and action you've chosen to take – that will allow you not just to survive the journey, but to thrive on the journey.

Working to become a champion, and experiencing all that comes with it again and again each day is a huge burden, and many people who've lost that loving feeling will walk away if or when that burden gets too heavy. But those who developed a deeper, stronger love, through their commitment and their sacrifice, have what they need to press on. They don't feel burdened by what they have to do; they feel fortunate that they *get to do* the difficult work that becoming a champion requires.

Our culture has perpetuated the idea that things should come easily, comfortably, and conveniently, and that doing something difficult is miserable. But when you've developed an authentic love for what you do, you recognize that doing something difficult can be fun. In fact, in many ways, doing something difficult – something you've really had to work and struggle and fight for – is actually more fun! Think back on your most meaningful wins and achievements. The ones at the top of the list are never the ones that've come easy.

The pride you feel when you accomplish something difficult, especially when you know it's important, gives you a feeling that no external recognition can match. It fuels that fire burning inside you and encourages you to step back in the arena and get back to work again. The champion recognizes that working to become your best is a huge, challenging responsibility. And while pain is inevitable, misery is optional.

Loving the Game – Development

Developing your love for the game might seem like a challenge, especially if you're focused only on that superficial *feeling* we've talked about already. Part of loving the game means working to maintain that feeling, no doubt about it. You've got to stay connected to why you started doing what you do in the first place – because you loved it. But when you shift your focus to the commitment and sacrifice that really defines the love of a champion, then you see that cultivating your love is a conscious choice to make.

Developing that commitment starts with a decision to intentionally embrace the process. We've talked already about the long road you're required to travel to become your best, in any area of life. Losers have a tendency to focus on the destination instead of the journey. They celebrate those at the top of the mountain without acknowledging the work it took to get there. They envy the prize that was won without recognizing the price that was paid. They want to skip the struggle and get straight to the fun stuff. When they discover that the process can't be skipped, skirted, or compromised, then it becomes easy to resent. And it's hard to love something you resent.

On the other hand, by committing to the process, champions have accepted the reality of the journey that must be taken, the price that must be paid, and the struggle that must be endured. They see clearly that there is no other way to attain excellence but the long, slow, sometimes painful way, by choosing to step into the arena each day. That's where champions have chosen to focus. They trust that each step of the journey, including this step, is refining them into their best selves. Committing to the process means using whatever happens today to help make you better.

Of course, winning is an important part of the champion's experience in the arena. Champions know and love the triumph of high achievement. But embracing the process means loving everything else that comes with the journey, too. The champion's face is marred with dust and sweat and blood, and believe it or not, he loves it. He loves the striving. The erring. Even the failing. By clarifying the important role that *every* experience plays in the refining process, the champion is capable of loving all of it. It's all a part of the journey.

So if champions choose to focus their attention on love, what do losers focus on? Usually fear. There is actually plenty for the loser to fear – plenty for any of us to fear, if we choose to focus our attention there. Maybe it's the fear of an unknown result or outcome. It could be the fear of looking bad. Maybe it's a fear of failure. No matter what you're afraid of, fear is always focused on an uncertain future. And the truth is, no amount of worry can change it. Fear robs you of the joy that's available – right here and right now – and instead paralyzes your performance.

That's why embracing the process is so important. Embracing the process takes our focus off what's uncontrollable – the future – and re-centers it on what is controllable – the present. Embracing the process means forgetting about what's to come, and focusing instead on stepping into the arena right where we are. It means striving valiantly to win this day. This hour. This moment. It means zooming in on being your best right where your feet are. This practice. This assignment. This drill. This conversation. This meeting.

A full commitment to the present moment drives out fear. It also prepares you most effectively for whatever outcome you may have been worried about in the first place. The best way to get the results you want is to forget about what's to come and simply be great right where you are – right here, right now. If you do that, you'll be as prepared as you can be when your big moment arrives.

Our level of commitment is one intentional choice we can make to exhibit and further develop our love. Our level of sacrifice is another. While commitment asks, "What are you willing to give?" sacrifice asks, "What are you willing to give up?" It's purposely surrendering an important thing in life for the sake of something you've determined is more important. Every time you choose to sacrifice – your time, your attention, or your convenience – you are doing more than simply saying you love the game. You are proving it.

Finally, you develop your Hidden Talent in this area when you choose to allow what you feel on the inside to reveal itself on the outside. You further cultivate your love for the game when you let your love show. Showing up with a bounce in your step and a smile on your face is proof of your passion. If you genuinely love it, then show it! It should be tough to contain. Clap your hands, or pump your fist, or give someone a high five. Spread that love! When you do, you not only fuel the fire burning inside your own heart, you also help fan the flames in those around you. Your infectious enthusiasm helps you be your best, and helps those around you do the same.

Loving the Game - Separation

When you intentionally work to connect with and more deeply cultivate your love for the game, you set yourself apart. In a world full of dull, lifeless people, those on fire have a tendency to stand out.

Loving the game makes you unique because it changes your perspective. When your heart's not in your work, it's easy to focus on the obligation you see before you. There's a lot of work that has to be done. But when you've cultivated your love for the game, it's easy to recognize the blessing before you. This isn't work that has to be done; it's work that *gets* to be done. You don't see the obligation; you see the opportunity.

When you have an opportunity perspective, you feel excited and inspired. You anticipate the day ahead and all that comes with it. You're focused and driven to do your best work. Despite the circumstances, there is an underlying sense of gratitude – that you are fortunate to be here, and thankful for this chance to play. You're feeling blessed instead of stressed.

For those with an obligation perspective, it's easy to feel burdened, fatigued, and frustrated. At best, you'll tolerate the day ahead and all that comes with it. With an attitude like that, even if you do the work that's required, what kind of standard will you create for yourself? It's hard to be great at what you do when you don't love what you do.

If you're the coach, the boss, or the leader of your group or organization, who would you rather have on your team? If you were the one who was ultimately judged, not just on your team's results but also on the standard of its performance, who would you choose to hand the biggest, most important work to? Who would you want by your side when it's time to step into the arena? I'll take the guy I can see is enthusiastic and seems grateful and excited to be here. I bet you'd say the same thing, and I bet your coach or boss would, too.

Beyond that, as the one in charge, would you really want to have to manage people who show up to work every day burdened, fatigued, and frustrated? You've got plenty to worry about already without constantly worrying about motivating the unmotivated. Leaders have an appreciation for those people who show up with energy and enthusiasm. Those are the people you want to be around, the people you want to reward, and the people you want to see succeed. When your coach or boss thinks of you, which category does he put you in?

Beyond the separation you create from those around you, loving the game also sets you apart in your pursuit of excellence – in working to reach your full potential. As you continue to live, work, and play from the heart, you create distance from who you used to be. That's because when you love what you do, your work flows from the inside-out. You don't need some rah-rah speech to get your motor running. You also don't need anyone else to set a standard for the quality of your work or confirm that your performance is good enough. When you love the game, you create your own standard. Instead of having to work to check just enough boxes to receive someone else's approval, you get to go on checking all the boxes you know you're capable of, regardless of who's watching.

If you're a loser, you probably do whatever's necessary when the coach or boss is standing over you, but when the person in charge is gone, your charade is over. Your effort diminishes. Your focus wanes. You haven't been working in an attempt to get better. You've been working in an attempt to get finished. As a worker, you should feel excited for a chance to compete in this work, not obligated just to complete it.

If you're a champion, who's watching over you is irrelevant to your pursuit. You're stepping into the arena to give your best in this moment for yourself, not for someone else. Your passion and commitment prove that. You may be able to fool someone else into thinking you've done the work, but you can't fool yourself. Deep in your heart, you always know the truth.

Loving the game is the foundation for building and developing every other Hidden Talent on the list. That's why we started here. In whatever areas of life you are working to become a champion, I hope you can uncover for yourself the reality of the challenging responsibility you face: this is not easy. You're gonna have to work and struggle and fight for it. Even still, you aren't meant to fear it, and you aren't meant to resent it. You're meant to love it, every part.

KEY CONCEPTS FOR
LOVING THE GAME

- Loving the Game is the foundation on which every other Hidden Talent is built. If you don't love it, you'll never be your best at it.

- Loving the Game means maintaining and staying connected to your passion for playing. You can do that by regularly remembering why you started doing this work in the first place.

- Loving the Game is also about a conscious choice, about a commitment you've made regardless of how you feel.

- Allow the love you feel on the inside to reveal itself on the outside.

- When you choose to focus on the opportunity instead of the obligation, your energy and enthusiasm naturally spring forth.

WHAT CHAMPIONS SAY ABOUT
LOVING THE GAME

"The only way to do great work is to love what you do." *-Steve Jobs*

"My motivation comes from playing the game I love." *-Lionel Messi*

"You can only get good if you love the game." *-Bobby Fischer*

"Nothing great was ever achieved without enthusiasm." *-Ralph Waldo Emerson*

"There is no such thing as a half-hearted champion." *-John Maxwell*

CHAPTER 8:

GIVING YOUR BEST

YOUR HIDDEN TALENT

Giving Your Best – Recognition

One thing that's important to recognize as we move forward is the crucial connection that so many Hidden Talent areas have with one another. Usually, when you commit to developing yourself in one area, you also positively impact another. At the same time, when you neglect an area, you very likely hinder your growth someplace else. Your improvement in each individual area is important, but they are all tied together.

Take the connection between loving the game and giving your best, for example. We talked in the previous chapter about the long, difficult journey it takes to become a champion. It's your love for the game that fuels you on that journey, and allowing that fire to go out makes giving everything you've got today much harder. But when you intentionally work to cultivate that love, you also increase your capacity to do the work – even the hardest work ahead of you. When your tank is full, you can go farther, harder, faster than when you're sitting on empty.

Hard work, not surprisingly, has gotten a bad rap amongst the losers. It's easy for losers to see this requirement – giving their best – as some sort of punishment. Jay Bilas refutes that point perfectly in his book, *Toughness*. He says, "Hard work is not punishment. Hard work is the price of admission for the opportunity to reach a standard of sustained excellence. No player has ever achieved sustained excellence without hard work." Sustained excellence. That's what the champion is chasing, right? Becoming your best requires giving your best. Champions recognize and accept this uncomfortable yet important reality.

That's not to say that losers won't work hard – they will. But there's a big difference between working hard and giving your best. Losers will work...when they think it's important. They want to win, just like everyone else, which is why they identify those times they believe work is necessary – usually on game day, or at crunch time, or some other time and place they've convinced themselves winning and losing is decided. Losers label those moments as important and significant, and they make sure to exert themselves fully when they believe the outcome's on the line.

The problem with this approach is that by labeling some moments as important and significant, the loser is also sometimes – maybe even inadvertently – labeling others as less important and less significant. What kind of work generally falls into the loser's "less important and less significant" category? It might be that work he or she thinks nobody will ever see. Or maybe it's the work they've labeled as boring, basic, or elementary – like, you know, the fundamentals. Remember Pablo Casals' champion-minded approach to the fundamentals? Losers don't recognize what champions see clearly: that often, excellence is forged in the fundamentals.

That's what makes champions like Casals different. They don't categorize moments by some skewed sense of significance. Embracing the process allows them to recognize an important reality that sets them apart, the reality that *every* moment matters. The champion sees the truth in that old adage, "how you do anything is how you do everything." This means that, in contrast to the loser's approach, there is actually great value in the work that nobody else will ever see. What might be considered boring, basic, or elementary gets the champion's full attention, because champions chase excellence even in the simple stuff.

You can be sure that both the loser and the champion will be ready to step into the arena on game night this Friday. In fact, it may be hard to tell them apart then. They'll both be giving their best. But only one of them is willing to step in the arena at practice Monday through Thursday. Losers foolishly diminish the significance of those early-week practices – "who cares, all we work on is the boring stuff" – and then just as foolishly believe they'll be able to flip the switch on their effort when they step into the spotlight.

Meanwhile, champions recognize that you play like you practice. Those early week practices, focused on the fundamentals, may seem routine or mundane – even boring, sometimes – but the champion recognizes that even on those days, there's an arena to be stepped into. Champions aren't hoping their effort rises to the occasion on game night; instead they're training their minds and bodies to play at full capacity every day. With an attitude like that, who do you think'll be more prepared to play their best when Friday night rolls around?

Champions recognize that developing this talent, this ability to give their best, is about building and developing their capacity for work, both physically and mentally. They give a singular effort – their very best, period. Losers, conversely, give what might be called a circumstantial effort. They give their best...until. Until it starts to hurt. Until it looks uncool. Until they think no one's watching.

Giving Your Best – Development

Physically, champions build and develop that capacity for work by intentionally pushing themselves outside their comfort zone. Champions have come to accept that physical discomfort is a required part of the experience; they're constantly choosing to push their limits. They are willing to fight through fatigue – even pain – as part of their pursuit. Champions are comfortable being uncomfortable.

Losers might work, but only when the conditions are right. They have a propensity to fold under the weight of fatigue and discomfort. They are easily victimized, like it's unfair that the work is so difficult or that they're required to endure it. They still haven't put those pieces of the puzzle together – that hard work isn't punishment, it's the cost of greatness. Losers are defined by their commitment to comfort. It keeps them out of the arena. It keeps them safe and clean. Sadly, it usually ends up keeping them from becoming their best.

Ultimately, stepping into the arena of development here means asking yourself a simple question, a question each of us faces wherever we are and whatever we're doing. The question is simply, "will you accept or justify that your current circumstances are enough to keep you from giving your best?" Every time you accept that, yes, you will allow your current circumstances to dictate your effort, you then become a victim to that circumstance. You choose to accept something less than your best, and in doing so you step out of the arena and away from your champion self. And each time you choose the loser's response, you also make it easier to justify giving in next time, often to an even weaker or less worthy challenge to come.

At the same time, every time you stand up and decide that you will not allow the circumstance you're facing to influence your effort – that you're committed to giving a singular effort, no matter what – you strengthen yourself for next time. The more you mindfully, intentionally, and exceptionally choose to give your best, no matter the situation, the more of a habit it becomes. With each winning choice, your talent grows, and you prepare yourself to step into an even bigger, more important arena and overcome an even bigger, more challenging circumstance next time.

So what circumstances will you allow yourself to become a victim to? What will you allow to keep you from giving your best? No matter what game you're playing today – in a packed arena under Friday night lights or alone with the fundamentals on a Monday afternoon – you'll have plenty of circumstances to face. Some may be physical:

-You are tired. Will you allow that circumstance to affect your ability to give your best?

-You are sore. Will you allow that circumstance to affect your ability to give your best?

-You are in pain. Will you allow that circumstance to affect your ability to give your best?

-You are limited in your God-given ability (you're shorter, you're slower, you're weaker, etc.) compared to those in this competition. Will you allow that circumstance to affect your ability to give your best?

-You are limited in your sport-specific skill (you're not as good a ball-handler, hitter, kicker, etc.) as those in this competition. Will you allow that circumstance to affect your ability to give your best?

Others may be mental:

-You are frustrated. Will you allow that circumstance to affect your ability to give your best?

-You are bored. Will you allow that circumstance to affect your ability to give your best?

-You feel you've been treated unfairly. Will you allow that circumstance to affect your ability to give your best?

-You didn't get something you thought you were entitled to. Will you allow that circumstance to affect your ability to give your best?

-You are clearly superior to your competition. Will you allow that circumstance to affect your ability to give your best?

-You are clearly inferior to your competition. Will you allow that circumstance to affect your ability to give your best?

-You are winning. Will you allow that circumstance to affect your ability to give your best?

-You are losing. Will you allow that circumstance to affect your ability to give your best?

There are more than just those listed here, but stop and think for a minute about the champions in your line of work. It doesn't matter what you do or what your arena looks like. You could be the star of the team or the last man on the bench. The expert in your field or the beginner. The CEO chasing excellence in your corner office during the day, or the janitor, chasing excellence as you intentionally, mindfully, and exceptionally clean that same office alone each night.

Champions on the playing field, at work, or at home have decided, at some point along the journey, that the answer to most or all of the questions listed above is "no." No, I will not allow being tired, or sore, or in pain to keep me from giving my best. No, I will not allow my frustration to keep me from giving my best. No, I will not allow the scoreboard, whatever it says, to keep me from giving my best. Champions give a singular effort. They don't allow the circumstances of their situation to determine the effort they give, and if you want to be a champion, neither can you.

Giving Your Best – Separation

In a world where most people give in when things get uncomfortable, those who've developed the ability to give their best in every situation stand out from the crowd. These are the people who have what Hall of Fame football coach Vince Lombardi called "a commitment to excellence." Average or mediocre people – the losers – they have an interest; but champions have a commitment. Can you see the separation that creates between them?

People who are interested give what they can, when they can. The problem with this approach is there's always a challenge, an obstacle, or an excuse for any of us to focus on if we look hard enough to find it. Because circumstances of life fluctuate from day to day, the loser's effort and engagement fluctuates from day to day, too. Losers are hard to count on because you never know exactly who you're gonna get when they walk through that door. The loser may be Dr. Jekyll today and Mr. Hyde tomorrow.

One day they show up fully engaged, committed, and ready to go. The next day, they're distant and distracted. One day focused, the next day flighty. They can give the team's best effort today and its worst tomorrow. They can treat people well one day and then treat those same people poorly the next. Their interest – and therefore their attitude, their focus, and their effort – are all circumstantial.

People who are committed to excellence are different. They give their very best no matter how they feel. That's not to say that champions don't have challenges, issues, or excuses available to them. It simply means they've determined that those circumstances won't be permitted to affect their effort or their focus. There's a level of constancy and consistency with champions, both mentally and physically, that separates them from everyone else. When the champion walks in the door, you know exactly who you're going to get. They are the same person every day.

Mentally, they show up ready to go. There's a focus that comes with a commitment to excellence. That's not to say they're never distracted or depressed or angry. But it does mean that when there's a job to do, champions can be counted on. They can focus up, set distractions aside, and give their full attention to the task at hand.

That same level of consistency is evident in their physical effort, too. It's hard to tell how champions feel on the inside based on the effort you see from them on the outside. A champion's effort looks just the same – awesome – no matter what they're feeling. When the loser is tired, angry, or hurting, it's usually obvious to an observer, but champions find a way to keep running full throttle no matter what's happening internally. They are never not hustling, pushing, and striving valiantly.

This is a big reason why champions win. How many people have given in to their circumstances, and therefore given up on some important pursuit in life just before breaking through to achievement? How many have walked away from the wall in front of them with a few swings still left in their hammer, assuming it was no use and their work would never come to fruition? Too many. Don't relegate yourself to this sorry group of regretful souls. It may well be that wall needs only your next swing of the hammer to crack and then crumble before you. Don't give up. Your big break is coming. Your opportunity is close. Keep hustling and keep trusting that what you'll get – and more importantly, who you'll become for your effort – will be worth the price you've paid.

Every time you stretch yourself in this Hidden Talent area, you create a new mark for your personal best that you weren't capable of reaching before. And even though sometimes really stretching yourself can hurt a little, it is fun to reach someplace you've never been. Plus, the more you stretch, the more flexible you become. You train yourself to work at a capacity you weren't capable of before. Experiencing this kind of growth spurs more growth. You get better at giving your best when you realize that your best has gotten better.

When you commit to this process and you develop your talent, you continue to set yourself apart. When things are quick, easy, and convenient, you'll find plenty of people in the arena competing for success. But as the challenging circumstances mount, the losers gradually start to fade, and when they give in, you can press on. The distance you create between yourself and everyone else is directly proportional to the effort you've conditioned yourself to give – in both the big moments and the small. The more you develop, the bigger and better the opportunities you find. The better the impression you make. And the more unique and uncommon you become.

KEY CONCEPTS FOR
GIVING YOUR BEST

- Hard work is not punishment. Simply put, it's the cost of greatness. Becoming your best requires giving your best.

- Champions give a singular effort – their very best, period. Losers give a circumstantial effort. They give their very best...until. Until it starts to hurt. Until it looks uncool. Until they think no one is watching.

- Champions push themselves outside their comfort zone. They are comfortable being uncomfortable.

- There's a level of constancy and consistency with champions, both mentally and physically, that separates them from everyone else.

- A champion's effort looks the same – awesome – no matter what they're feeling.

WHAT CHAMPIONS SAY ABOUT
GIVING YOUR BEST

"Hustle is a talent." *-Bill Russell*

"I think the thing was I was always willing to work; I was not the fastest or the biggest player but I was determined to be the best football player I could be on the football field, and I think I was able to accomplish that through hard work." *-Jerry Rice*

"There may be people that have more talent than you. But there's no excuse for anyone to work harder than you." *-Derek Jeter*

"The reason a lot of people don't recognize opportunity is because it usually goes around wearing overalls and looking like hard work." *-Thomas Edison*

"No one who ever gave his best regretted it." *-George Halas*

CHAPTER 9:

OVERCOMING ADVERSITY

YOUR HIDDEN TALENT

Overcoming Adversity – Recognition

There are so many qualities that separate the champion from everyone else. As we've noted already, it might be their passion. It could be their effort. There are plenty more important separators to come, too. But no talent creates a wider gap between the winners and the losers than the one separating them in this specific area: the champion's ability to overcome adversity.

Champions have come to recognize some important realities about chasing excellence in any area. They recognize that anything that's really worth doing in life will have to be done despite some challenge, struggle, or hardship. If winning, or success, or excellence were easy, then everyone would do it, but the truth is it's not easy. It requires a significant price to pay, and the champion has accepted that adversity is built into that price – it's part of the deal.

The road to greatness is long and hard. The daily challenges you'll be forced to face and overcome on that road will go largely unnoticed by others. Most days you'll have to give up many of the comforts and conveniences your peers take for granted. You'll have to perform, over and over again in the dark, before your hard work is ever revealed for the world to see. And even then, you may have to fail repeatedly before you ever succeed.

Recognizing and accepting these realities change how champions envision the road ahead. This perspective gives them the foresight to see the truth, that this isn't gonna be some cakewalk to the top. There will be plenty of unexpected twists and turns – maybe some detours and even a few roadblocks – on the way to their destination.

So, it's worth asking: have you recognized and accepted that challenge, struggle, and hardship will be a part of your journey? Have you included the twists and turns, the detours and even the roadblocks that are all a part of your path to greatness? There's no way any of us can know what exactly that adversity will look like, when it will appear, or how it will complicate the goals we've set out to achieve, but recognizing it as a part of our story does help us prepare to rise up and meet it when it arrives.

By recognizing the important role adversity plays in any success story, you can dismiss the notion that the challenges you face are meant to define you. Instead, you see that your challenges actually refine you into the resilient, tough-minded person that being your best requires you to be. When your stellar season is suddenly sidetracked by an unexpected injury, or you're blindsided by your boss's unexpected decision, or your own bad judgment screws up your plans, you don't have to fall to pieces. When you recognize that struggle is a necessary part of any success story – including your own – you can embrace it as an opportunity to prove you've got what it takes to win.

Losers have a different perspective. They aren't capable of rising up and meeting adversity this way, usually because they haven't recognized the important place it has to have in their success story. Losers believe there are big, important things for them to do in the world, but they haven't included challenge, struggle, or hardship as a part of the story. They've constructed for themselves a naïve picture of that cakewalk to the top. Instead of spending time preparing to meet and overcome adversity, losers expect that it'll just magically avoid them. When it doesn't, it's easy for them to accept the roadblock ahead of them as the sad end to their story.

Clarifying adversity's place in the story empowers the champions. They recognize that it's not the challenge that defines them, but their response to that challenge, and what they accomplish in spite of it. Losers crumble when things get tough. Because they see failure as the end of the road, it's easy to fear it or fear being defined by it. Here's another example of the fear that cripples or paralyzes the loser. It breeds an unhealthy victim mentality, that life's not fair or they haven't gotten what they're entitled to. By failing to recognize the reality of the path, losers complicate the journey.

Champions also recognize the critical role that this ability – overcoming adversity – plays in helping them become their best. The truth is, a person can have every advantage in the world – more God-given talent, better resources, better equipment, and better training. But if every time things get hard, that person crumbles to pieces? Then how important, really, is all that stuff? How valuable are all the pretty fixtures in a fancy house if the foundation's weak and fragile? In truth, none of the other stuff matters without a strong, sturdy foundation of toughness that fortifies everything else.

At the same time, even with less natural ability, fewer resources, mediocre equipment and moderate training, developing a high-level toughness gives you the opportunity to win whatever game you find yourself in. If you possess real toughness, what you don't possess becomes much less important. If you're serious about becoming your best and you recognize this reality, then only one question remains…how can you afford not to develop it?

Overcoming Adversity – Development

Like every Hidden Talent area, developing your ability to overcome adversity is a long, difficult, sometimes painful process. That process begins with the winning choice you make to step into the arena today. When you do that – when you intentionally decide to get to work on getting tougher – you realize that this development work isn't necessarily new. It's a lot like work you've done before.

Consider the way your body elevates its toughness level, let's say, through the process of working with your hands. If you do any kind of regular work with your hands – like routinely using a baseball bat, a dumbbell, or a garden tool, for instance – you've probably developed some toughness where you need it. Your body naturally recognizes that there are places it's required. Your skin gets strong and callused, so you can handle when the work gets tough again. It's not a quick or painless process, but exposing your hands to some difficult work helps you become more resilient for next time. This is how each of us were designed.

If you haven't developed toughness where you need it, the hard work will painfully expose the important places you're too weak or too sensitive. Throw on some gloves and you can protect yourself from the friction that might cause you to blister, but if you want to get tough, you've got to take the gloves off and allow that toughness to develop. Our hands don't get tough by luck or by accident or by wishful thinking. They get tough by doing tough things.

The same is true for you and your mental toughness. Developing the resilience it takes to handle challenges and adversity doesn't happen by luck or by accident or by wishful thinking. You get tough by doing tough things. You can protect yourself from the pain of exposure – the "friction" in life – if you're so determined, but if you want your toughness to develop, you've got to take the gloves off and go through the strengthening process. That's the winning choice you have to make, the arena you're required to step into. When you make that decision, to intentionally start getting exposed, then your toughness starts getting developed.

If you have a desire to do something big and important in life – to become a champion where it really matters – then there'll be plenty of opportunities for you to get exposed, blistered, and even wounded by adversity. Early in the process, it may happen a lot. As you may have noticed in your experience already, things rarely go as planned. Challenge, struggle, and hardship are *always* a part of the story, remember? The game is played by imperfect people, including you. You will swing and miss. You will make some bone-headed decisions. You'll be subjected to some unfair calls. You'll be sick or tired or sore. There are always challenges when you play the game. Always. Some will be your fault and some won't, but regardless of what the difficulties are or why they exist, champions have developed the resilience to overcome.

If you don't have that resilience yet, then you have a choice when adversity hits. You can put those gloves of protection on and do what you can to protect yourself – you can find someone or something to blame for your trouble, make excuses for why the task is too difficult, or justify how you've been unfairly cheated out of an easy road to success.

Or you can step into the arena and face this foe. You can embrace the truth about this roadblock before you: that anything that's really worth doing in life, including this thing, must be done despite some challenge, struggle, or hardship. That your response to this adversity is actually much more important than the adversity itself. And that if you've developed the toughness it takes to overcome this adversity, then despite whatever it is you might not have, you've got enough to win.

The first time you rise up to meet your challenge, it's probably gonna hurt. You'll probably blister, and even bleed a little. But your experience in the arena today will make you stronger and more prepared to meet an even bigger challenge tomorrow. Every time you take the champion's approach to adversity you develop your resilience, you cast yet another vote for your champion self, and you make toughness a bigger part of your identity.

Now, do you need to experience every hardship in life? No, probably not. We don't need our hands to be callused everywhere. In fact, for them to be their best, some parts of our hands need to be more sensitive and receptive. Our minds work the same way. If you are hard and calloused all the time and in every situation, you'll miss some opportunities that require you to be more sensitive and receptive. But if you want to be a champion, you better be able to handle the friction that comes with chasing excellence. Figure out what it is that you really want to do and where in that pursuit your toughness will be required, then take the gloves off and get to work.

Overcoming Adversity – Separation

The more you develop your ability to overcome adversity, the stronger, more resilient, and more unique it makes you. Once you've uncovered where exactly your toughness is required, and then you commit to the process of rising up to meet it head on and trusting in the process of development, you get better. You separate yourself from those who don't have it, and you give yourself unique opportunities because you're capable of staying in the arena and fighting for longer.

Consider all the ways adversity can wound you. Maybe it's a mistake you've made that knocks you down. Maybe it's a teammate's mistake. Maybe you've done your best but come up short, or you're facing criticism – either fairly or unfairly – about your performance. Maybe it's just a bad break that's come flying in your direction. Whatever it is, if you're performing at a high level, adversity is everywhere. Sometimes you see it coming and sometimes you don't, but it's always there, threatening to expose you and anyone else who's not prepared to take a hit.

By developing your toughness, you've learned how to do just that: take a hit. Inevitably it's coming. A mistake gets made, and with it the piercing blow it delivers. All around you, it's wounding people – taking them out of their game, messing with their minds, bringing them to their knees. But if you're a champion, what you've developed makes you bulletproof. Adversity's knocked some people down. Knocked others out. But it doesn't destroy you. You can keep moving forward.

How else does this ability make you unique? It allows you to play in the present – to focus completely on the winning moment you're in. In the arena, there's no controlling what's already happened. The past is over and done with. There's also no controlling what's yet to happen – the future can't be determined until it arrives. The only thing you can control is the here and now, and that *should be* all that matters. Unfortunately for most people, it isn't.

Most people are easily wounded by adversity, and they struggle to move past it. Their performance in the current moment is negatively affected by something that's happened in a previous moment. Their lack of toughness keeps them from moving past the mistake, or the criticism, or the bad break – whatever it was. So instead of being all-in right here in the moment they can control, they spend their time thinking about, worrying about, or dwelling on something that's already done. Adversity wounds them in the moment, and then continues to hurt their performance long after.

As a champion, however, you are different. You are unique in your ability to constantly play in the present – to give your best to *this* winning moment. Since you aren't easily wounded by adversity, you don't have to spend your time and energy trying to recover. You can quickly move on from whatever's happened and concentrate on what's most important – winning the battle that's right in front of you.

Finally, developing this Hidden Talent gives you the uncommon ability to win even when conditions aren't ideal. When you hear about a team or an athlete who wins ugly, it usually means that for whatever reason, things haven't gone according to the plan. They haven't played particularly well, they've made a lot of mistakes, or they've had to overcome a lot of adversity in order to succeed. Nobody plans on going out and winning ugly, but sometimes for the champion, that's what it takes.

Losers usually don't possess the fortitude it takes to win ugly. When things get ugly, losers usually start to break down. Of course, when things are easy, comfortable and convenient? No problem. The loser will be right there competing. But when the challenges inevitably arise, their weak and fragile nature is revealed.

For the champion, just because some days success is hard to find doesn't mean it can't be found. In fact, with the right perspective, winning ugly can actually be pretty fun, especially when you realize that not everyone's capable of doing it. It's just another way champions separate themselves from everyone else.

Like every Hidden Talent, the separation you create – not just with others in your pursuit of success, but with your old self as you continue to chase excellence – continues to grow over time. The more you step into the arena, and the more you develop your Hidden Talent, the more set apart you become. There's no final round bell in this fight you're fighting, which means you can continue to get tougher and tougher, and prepare yourself to step into bigger and more important arenas forever. If you stick to the process, there's no telling what challenges you might eventually overcome.

That's good news, because there's also no telling what challenges you may have to face moving forward. Only you know the fights you've had to fight up until now, but you can bet there will be bigger, more meaningful fights to come in your future. It's hard to say when or where, or even why. Sometimes, life is hard because we've made it hard. Our own bad judgment or poor decisions have put us in a tough spot. Other times, life's hard because...well, just because. We haven't caused it to happen, it's just happened. Sometimes it's completely unfair that adversity exists and it's just as impossible to explain why.

You'll probably experience plenty of both kinds of adversity in your life, and the work you're doing today is preparing you to be your best then, when your best will really be needed. If the adversity you're facing is your own fault, you'll be trained to rise up and meet it. You can find the strength to fight for making it right, the fortitude to accept the weight of responsibility, and the toughness to keep on moving forward in spite of the struggle. If the adversity you're facing isn't your fault, you'll find you're trained to face it and fight it all the same. If you've done the work it takes to become a champion, then in your moment of adversity, you'll do what champions do. Dig deep. Look that challenge square in the eye. Step into the arena. And fight.

KEY CONCEPTS FOR
OVERCOMING ADVERSITY

- Becoming a champion requires a significant price to pay, and the champion has accepted that adversity is built into that price.

- Challenges aren't meant to define you; they're meant to refine you into the resilient, tough-minded person that being your best requires you to be.

- Every time you take the champion's approach to adversity, you develop your resilience, you cast yet another vote for your champion self, and you make toughness a bigger part of your identity.

- Champions are able to play in the present – to give their best to *this* winning moment.

- Losers usually don't possess the fortitude to win ugly. But for the champion, just because some days success is hard to find doesn't mean it can't be found.

WHAT CHAMPIONS SAY ABOUT
OVERCOMING ADVERSITY

"If you're trying to achieve, there will be roadblocks. I've had them, everybody's had them. But obstacles don't have to stop you. If you run into a wall, don't turn around and give up. Figure out how to climb it, work through it, or go around it." *-Michael Jordan*

"The game honors toughness." *-Brad Stevens*

"I think sometimes in life the biggest challenges end up being the best things that happen in life." *-Tom Brady*

"The measure of who we are is how we react to something that doesn't go our way."
-Gregg Popovich

"Adversity introduces a man to himself."
-Albert Einstein

CHAPTER 10:

SEEKING IMPROVEMENT

YOUR HIDDEN TALENT

Seeking Improvement – Recognition

Champions aren't born, they're built. That's the foundation of this book, that when you dig deep to uncover what makes a champion a champion, you find that those we consider excellent in their chosen field haven't been born great, they haven't gotten great by accident, and they haven't won *and then* become great. There are characteristics that champions share – gifts they've recognized, chosen to develop, and used to separate themselves from everyone else. Champions have been built on purpose over time. They've put in the time and the work it takes to become champions, and that's why they win.

The problem is, what we want these days, we've been conditioned to expect we can get right away. As we've said already, our society places a premium on what comes easily, conveniently, and comfortably – that's the world we live in. Anything that takes time to build or develop these days usually gets labeled as flawed or obsolete. This line of thinking has filtered its way into our perspective on almost everything we look at, including ourselves.

Despite the long process that's required to become our best, it's easy to make snap judgments about who we are or what we can do based only on what we see right in front of us. Some people just have what it takes to be a champion, we naively justify, and some people don't. This is a loser's belief. When we buy into it, we turn our attention away from what matters most — that ever-important process of learning, growing, and getting better, and instead turn our attention toward things that matter less — usually an unhealthy and unproductive emphasis on ranking, judgment, or comparison.

When you're focused on rankings, judgment, and comparison, your primary goal isn't getting better, it's looking good. You'll do whatever you can to build and maintain a facade of perfection. You have to, since your entire identity is built on how you look. People with this perspective usually spend their time avoiding struggle or challenge at all costs and focusing their time and attention on what comes easy. That façade of perfection sabotages their opportunities for growth and makes looking good — or at least doing whatever's necessary not to look bad — all that matters.

When you're focused on becoming a champion, not surprisingly, your priorities change. Your primary goal isn't looking good. Your primary goal is stepping into the arena today and competing, wherever you are and whatever you're doing, and using the experience to get better. As a champion, you know the man in the arena is no picture of perfection. The fact is, truly competing isn't always pretty. You're gonna get dirty and sweaty and bloody, just like Roosevelt promised.

And for what result? Who knows. You might win, you might not. But regardless of the outcome, you're committed to the process of using whatever happens today, so you can prepare yourself to win for tomorrow.

Champions recognize that the best never stop getting better. They see every experience as an opportunity to learn and grow. In any work that we do, but especially here in these Hidden Talent areas, there's no way to know how much we can improve or where exactly that improvement might end up taking us. Champions recognize that they *can* get better. That they *should*. That they *must*.

For the loser, a focus on rankings, comparison, and judgment discourages improvement. Losers typically aren't focused on how good they can get; they're usually focused on how much better they are than someone else. It's easier, more convenient, and more comfortable for any of us to highlight our strengths than it is to focus on our weaknesses. But the more clearly you recognize that improvement is possible (and necessary), the less interested you become in anyone else. Chasing excellence means becoming the very best *you* can be – that's the standard the champion is committed to. It's the standard that drives the best of the best in any field.

When Michael Jordan was the most dominant basketball player on earth, he spent his off-seasons working to add some new scoring move to his already unstoppable arsenal. Tom Brady, years into his Hall of Fame career and already cemented as one of the game's greatest quarterbacks, still focused his pre-season workouts on the elementary footwork he learned as a young player. And Wayne Gretzky, aka "The Great One" of hockey, frequently stayed after practice, alone on the rink, working to improve a specific shot that many believed he had already perfected.

If anyone had the right to kick back, relax, and enjoy being on top, it should've been these guys, right? They were the best to ever do what they did. *The best!* And yet, for each of these champion athletes, who they were was less important to them than who they believed they could become. Their pursuit of excellence never involved any ranking, judgment, or comparison. There's a lesson we can learn, and a mindset we can model, from their attitude towards improvement.

Of course, you're probably not Jordan or Brady or Gretzky. In fact, it may be easy for you to recognize that you aren't the best, maybe even by a long-shot. Those of us in this club face a different challenge. In this world of rankings, judgment, and comparison, it may be easy for us to think that people like those guys just have it, and people like us just don't. Your mediocre self whispers, "It doesn't matter what you do. You just aren't good enough." Or "You stink, so why even try?" These days it's easy to believe that if something doesn't come easy, then there's no use trying. When you stink, trying just makes you look foolish.

Please recognize those words for what they are – lies perpetuated by losers, maybe even by the loser inside you. It's easier, more convenient, and more comfortable for losers to accept mediocrity than it is to relentlessly seek improvement. But champions recognize that just because you aren't good at something right away doesn't mean you never will be. The loser, focused on some unhealthy judgment, says, "I just don't have it." The champion, focused instead on the process of growth and development, says, "I just don't have it...yet."

Champions recognize that even the expert was once a beginner.

Seeking Improvement – Development

So how do you get better at getting better? Once you recognize that you've been given this gift – the ability to improve – how do you use it to separate yourself, not just from those around you, but more importantly, from the person you used to be? Getting better is not for the faint of heart, so you better gear up. Your arena is waiting.

The truth is, improving is hard. It's the ultimate process-oriented work. Getting better requires you to give your very best. It takes an all-in commitment – giving your effort, your time, and your attention. It also takes all-out sacrifice. You've got to give up your pride. Give up your comfort and your convenience. Give up your need for acknowledgement and recognition. Once you've done all that – given *and* given up all that's required – you'll start seeing returns. You know what improvement gives you in return for all that you've given and given up? A barely noticeable speck of growth. And the sobering promise that earning another speck tomorrow will require even more commitment and more sacrifice than it did today.

Compare for a minute that reality of how improvement happens with the cultural mindset we described earlier, the one that's conditioned us to expect that what we want, we can get right away. This contrast – the one that exists between the harsh reality of what excellence requires and the false one we construct in our minds – is the reason stepping into the arena here is so difficult. You've got to give so much, and give up so much, to get so little in return. On its own, your decision today to step into the arena of improvement might not seem like it's worth the effort.

But when you commit to trusting the process and seeing the big picture, you see today in the context of all your yesterdays and tomorrows. It's not that champions don't wish the process of improvement was easier, but they have accepted that this is the reality of the path to greatness. And even though a speck of growth today isn't much, when you start sticking those specks together, over and over again each day, you create something more substantial. This is how improvement happens.

As always, your development in this area starts with a winning choice. Champions have chosen to show up today expecting to grow and change. They anticipate that opportunities to improve will exist in this experience today, and they're prepared and committed to search for them, identify them, and use them to get better. They are intentional in their approach to improvement; they get better on purpose. It's what researcher K. Anders Ericcson calls "deliberate practice." He defines it as "practice that focuses on tasks beyond your current level of competence and comfort."

Ericsson explains further. "Not all practice makes perfect," he says. "When most people practice, they focus on the things they already know how to do. Deliberate practice is different. It entails considerable, specific, and sustained efforts to do something you *can't* do well – or even at all." This is how champions seek improvement, focusing not on what they already know, but constantly stepping into that bigger, more challenging arena of work they can't do well, or at all. If you really want to get better, this is how Ericsson is encouraging you to practice as well.

This is not how most people approach this challenging work. Most people just go through the motions; when it comes to practice, they simply check the box and get it over with. They clock in, mindlessly do the required work, and clock out. Often, even those who work hard aren't showing up really expecting to grow and change. They aren't anticipating opportunities to improve today, and they aren't prepared or committed to searching for them, identifying them, and using them to get better. They aren't intentionally working to move beyond their current level of competence and comfort. For most, it's easier to accept what they don't have than it is to do the hard work that improvement requires.

The truth is, in whatever area we are working or playing today, most of us are waiting to get something we want. Who knows what waiting might look like for you. Maybe you think you should be a starter, but coach has you coming off the bench for now. Maybe you want to hit at the top of the lineup, but you've been penciled in closer to the bottom. Maybe you're an emerging star, but right now you've been asked to take a backseat to the team's current star. Unfortunately, you don't always get what you want. Sometimes you can and will get it, just not yet. In that instance, the question becomes…what will you do while you wait? The answer says a lot about who you are.

As you might expect, in this situation the champion makes a winning choice. He chooses to rise up and meet this challenge, to focus on what's important, and to control what's controllable: getting better. The champion continues to give his best and be a great teammate as a sub until his time to be a starter comes. Then, when it does, he'll be prepared to take advantage. If the champion finds himself hitting at the bottom of the lineup, he's determined to hit so well that coach will have to take notice. If coach does notice and he gets a shot at the top of the order, he'll be ready. If not, he'll keep hammering away where he is. And instead of worrying about whether or not he's identified as the star, the champion will keep on chasing excellence wherever he finds himself. Then, when it is his turn to step into the spotlight, he'll know he prepared the right way in the dark.

Instead of getting better, losers usually get bitter. After all, it's a lot easier to be critical, blame the coach, and sulk as a sub than it is to keep proving yourself every day. Instead of getting determined to hit better at the bottom of the lineup, it's easier to slide into a slump and then pout about it after. Instead of working and waiting to become the star, it's easier to turn jealous and resentful of the player ahead of you. Maybe, eventually the losers will get their chance in the spotlight. But even then, after having wasted their opportunities to improve, how prepared will they be?

If you're waiting to get what you want, remember it's not that you aren't good enough. It's that you aren't good enough...yet. Even if it's not the one you want or think you're entitled to, there's still an arena for you to step into, right where you are today. Stay in the fight, and keep getting better. Remember, no matter what you end up getting for your hard work, you'll be proud of what it helps you become.

Seeking Improvement – Separation

Hall of Fame football coach Lou Holtz famously said, "If you're not growing, you're dying." That means our character and our identity don't possess a neutral gear. Each day the choices we make are moving us forward or backward; we are improving ourselves or we are diminishing ourselves. If we aren't routinely challenging our inner champion to practice deliberately in the important areas of life – to keep learning and finding new ways to expand who we are and what we're about – then a part of us is gradually rotting away. The problem is that typically, just as growth happens slowly and deliberately, so death happens, too. By practicing deliberately, the champion has created only a speck of separation from the loser today, but over time, the gap between those who are growing and those who are dying becomes abundantly clear.

All living things work this way. If you stop watering a house plant today, for instance, it won't be dead tomorrow. In fact, it probably won't look any different at all. For days or even weeks, from the outside, that plant will look like it's always looked – green, healthy, alive. But inside, it's dying. And at some point, the damage that's been done on the inside will start to become evident on the surface. It won't be recoverable. It'll be weak and vulnerable, and only a fragment of what it once was, or what it was capable of becoming. The same can be said for each of us.

We need challenges in life, things to learn and stuff to work on. If we stop seeking improvement and just accept that we are now all that we'll ever be, or that we've done all that we're going to do – that there's nothing more out there for us to learn, achieve, or attain – then we start the process of dying inside. Like the houseplant, we may not look that different outwardly. For a time, we can fool people on the surface; they may not even notice the change. But when that happens – if we allow it to happen – our slow rot begins. And then, sadly, we too will be only a fragment of who we once were, or who we were capable of becoming.

Don't be fooled by improvement's seemingly insignificant impact today. Yes, the best you can do is a speck's worth of growth – maybe a little more if you really get after it. And yes, in the eyes of a world enamored with instant gratification and immediate judgment, that speck may not seem like it's worth all the work. But as a champion, you've become a bona fide speck collector. You're hunting them, tracking them down, and utilizing every opportunity you can to improve. You see the big picture, and you know that over time, it's your improvement that separates you. It sets you apart from those you're competing with and against. But more importantly, it sets you apart from who you used to be, and keeps moving you forward toward your very best.

KEY CONCEPTS FOR
SEEKING
IMPROVEMENT

- Our culture has placed a premium on what comes easily, conveniently, and comfortably. When we buy into it, we turn our attention away from what matters most – that ever-important process of learning, growing, and getting better, and instead turn our attention toward what matters less – usually an unhealthy emphasis on ranking, judgment, or comparison.

- The man in the arena is not focused on perfection; he's focused on improvement.

- Just because you aren't good at something right away doesn't mean you never will be. Even the expert was once a beginner.

- Champions are intentional in their approach to improvement. They get better on purpose.

- Our character and our identity don't possess a neutral gear. Each day the choices we make are moving us forward or backward. We are improving ourselves or we are diminishing ourselves.

WHAT CHAMPIONS SAY ABOUT
SEEKING
IMPROVEMENT

"Unless you try to do something beyond what you have already mastered, you will never grow. Every job is a self-portrait of the person who did it. Autograph your work with excellence."
-Vince Lombardi

"An ounce of practice is worth more than tons of preaching." *-Ghandi*

"Greatness always has its eye on improvement."
-Don Yeager

"Practice isn't the thing you do once you're good. It's the thing you do that makes you good." *-Malcolm Gladwell*

"Everything is practice." *-Pele*

CHAPTER 11:

GETTING COACHED

YOUR HIDDEN TALENT

Getting Coached – Recognition

One important part of becoming a champion is recognizing how many circumstances there are that can challenge your commitment to stepping in the arena. There's no denying that all those circumstances *will be* a part of the story you choose to write. And while you play the lead in your story, many other people will play a prominent role in what happens. Uncovering the truth about their place alongside you, the challenges they can create, and the opportunities they present is an important part of becoming your best.

Among those many secondary characters in your story, perhaps no one will play a more prominent role than your coach. For most of us, we'll be working under a boss for most of our lives. While some people are lucky enough to enjoy a healthy, productive relationship with their coach, others struggle through a more challenging dynamic. Regardless, we can all agree that getting coached can be a complicated experience.

Sometimes the experience can scramble our story. Coaching can easily feel negative, critical, or judgmental. It can seem unfair. But champions recognize not only that they're capable of getting coached, but that the experience is so important to the process of reaching their full potential. By recognizing and then developing this talent, champions help set themselves apart from the crowd. The same is true for you. This Hidden Talent helps you get better, and it opens doors – doors that remain closed for those who can't take advantage of getting coached.

Despite the huge individual responsibility that each one of us bears in becoming our very best, champions recognize that we cannot be our best without help. Wherever it is you dream about going, and whoever it is that you envision yourself being when you arrive at your destination, the truth is you cannot get there alone. No one gets there alone. Champions see clearly the important role a coach can play in helping them get better.

At the same time, champions recognize that getting coached isn't really about the coach. Sure, he or she may play an important role in your story, but this is *your* story. No matter what your coach chooses to do or say, who you are and who you become will be determined by your response. Many people feel defensive or victimized by the honesty of authentic coaching, but champions have uncovered a more powerful and productive reality.

The reality is that a coach who's on you – who has a high standard for your performance and who won't allow you to settle for anything less than your best – is a blessing, not a curse. If your coach is never coaching, instructing, or even criticizing you, that probably means one of two things: either he or she doesn't care about your performance and your improvement, or he or she doesn't think you have much to offer. If you're serious about becoming your best, then you recognize that despite the challenges it can present, having a real coach who's committed to really coaching isn't a burden. It's actually a benefit.

As we described in detail back in Chapter 10, champions are relentlessly driven by the process of improvement. They have the humility to accept that information from others – including their coach – is a valuable resource they can use to get better. As opposed to the proud, egotistical "know-it-all" attitude of the loser, champions are hungry for help in their pursuit of greatness. You might call them the "learn-it-all" type. That's really what they're after – learning all they can – and they trust that their coach can help. Champions don't feel defensive or victimized by their coach's honesty, even if it does seem critical. In fact, they crave information that can help them improve. That's why champions get coached.

Of course, just as there are champions and there are losers in every walk of life, so too are there champions and losers in coaching. Hopefully the coaches in your life are chasing excellence for themselves. Hopefully they recognize that there is an arena they are responsible for stepping into today, and that they've accepted the challenge that comes with a commitment to being their best. If your coach isn't a champion, it obviously that creates a uniquely formidable arena for you to step into.

But even if your coach is a champion – even if he or she is stepping into the arena for themselves each day – don't forget that they aren't perfect. As Roosevelt said, the man in the arena errs. He comes short again and again. Your coach will inevitably make decisions you don't like, say something that cuts you deep, or somehow complicate the success story you're trying to write. Maybe it'll be a mistake they've made that you'll have to overcome. Maybe it'll be a mistake you've made that you just don't want to accept. Sometimes it's tough to hear the cold, hard truth, but it's part of what getting coached requires.

I hope you can recognize that every event or experience, even the one with a coach that could be perceived as challenging or difficult, is an opportunity for you to get better. I hope you recognize that getting coached is a lot less about who your coach is and a lot more about who you are and what you're after. I hope you recognize that by developing this Hidden Talent, it helps you get better, and opens doors – doors that remain closed for those who can't get coached. I hope you recognize that getting coached helps you write the best version of your story, one you can be proud of.

Getting Coached – Development

Developing your ability to get coached starts with recognizing that you can get better, and that coaching can provide information that will help in your pursuit. That recognition helps clarify the choices – and eventually the habits – that lead to growth in this area, because it cultivates the humility that getting coached requires.

As is always the case, this process of development starts internally. You have some important questions to answer when it comes to growing and improving in this area. First, and most importantly, is this: am I willing to trust my coach? Any authentic relationship, especially one that can withstand the burden of honesty and authenticity in a competitive environment, requires trust. Depending on who you are and what you've experienced in your life, that arena – the trust arena – may be one of the biggest and most challenging for you to step into, but the bottom line is, you can't get coached if you aren't willing to trust your coach. Obviously he or she has a major say in building that trust, but you play an important part, too. The more you intentionally choose a willingness to trust, and the humility that comes with it, the more you exhibit your desire to learn. And the more you make coachability part of your character and identity.

Developing this Hidden Talent means cultivating not only your ability to trust, but also your ability to earn it in return. The most productive player-coach relationships are the ones where trust is both humbly chosen and intentionally earned by both sides on a regular basis. When it comes to the biggest assignments, the crunch-time moments, and the most important opportunities of the game, who will your coach choose to step on stage? The ones he or she can trust to perform.

So how do you develop your trustworthiness? First, through obedience. You earn trust by doing what you're supposed to do. If coach says, "here's what it takes to win, now go execute," there will likely be one of two responses from those under his direction. The arrogant "know-it-all" type might ignore coach's mandate or dismiss the instruction and works hard to justify doing it his own way. The humble, "learn-it-all" type has chosen to trust his coach, and, whether he loves the role he's been given or not, has chosen to step into the arena in front of him and be a star in that role. Whatever job he has, the champion is committed to doing like a champion. He knows that proving he can be trusted in his current role is the best way to prove he's ready for a bigger role. He listens and obeys. Take a minute to imagine that you're the coach. With all that's riding on your team's performance, which of these two players – the "know-it-all" or the "learn-it-all" – would you want in the game?

Obedience is important because obedience breeds discipline. Discipline is a requirement for anyone hoping to reach their full potential. That's because, in truth, the path that leads to becoming your best is narrow. Champions make winning choices in part by recognizing that if they want to be great, they don't have a lot of choices. You can't just do anything and become great – that's a loser's belief. Champions recognize the reality of the narrow path to excellence, and then more importantly, they have the discipline to stay on that path, despite the many distractions working to pull them away.

The disciplined player is a trustworthy player. And ironically, those who've developed their discipline actually end up finding more responsibility, more opportunity, and more freedom than those who haven't. Why? Because they can be trusted. The game always has a way of honoring those who do it right. And the beauty of this process is that this cycle of trust builds on itself. When you humbly choose to trust your coach, you develop your obedience. By developing your obedience, you develop your discipline. And developing your discipline builds your trustworthiness. This is the never-ending process of growing, improving, and developing your Hidden Talent.

As is usually the case, what you've chosen to develop on the inside has a way of showing itself on the outside. How you choose to act is a reflection of who you've chosen to become. Cultivating this Hidden Talent means developing more than just your internal desire to get coached; it means developing your external response to instruction as well. There are a few simple things you can do to prove you're serious about getting coached.

Eye contact, for instance, is an external response that demonstrates your internal desire. Looking someone in the eye while they're speaking is a simple signal that the speaker's message is being received. A head nod or some other non-verbal acknowledgement is another way to show you're interested in listening and learning, and that you've gotten the message loud and clear.

"Know-it-alls" have a way, either intentionally or not, of sending their coach the opposite message. Have you had a conversation with someone and you got the sense they weren't listening? Usually a lack of eye contact helps confirm that message. Looking somewhere else or gazing distractedly off into space doesn't send the message to your coach, "I'm all in." Usually that message relayed is more like "I'm bored" or "this doesn't really matter to me." Most of the time, whether or not you like the message being relayed is less important than whether or not it needs to and deserves to be heard.

Especially when things get tough, your external response to coaching is important. If you're planning to play, work, or perform at a high level, then you'll be dealing with others – including your coach – who've made a major investment in your performance. Emotions run high when something important's at stake, and you better expect that at some point, an angry coach will be part of your experience.

If your coach is angry, it's probably because something important's on the line. You need to see that something important's on the line for you in this moment, too. There's an arena to step into. Work hard to hear what is probably a rational message from what is possibly, in that emotional moment, an irrational messenger. If coach comes down hard on you, don't get depressed. Get determined! Use the emotion of the moment positively by digging deep and elevating your game. Champions can handle tough coaching. Look your coach in the eye and prove you can handle it, too. When you do, you not only improve yourself by accepting information that helps you get better, you also make an important statement to your coach about your high level of toughness and trust.

Not surprisingly, losers crumble when the coaching gets tough. They can't hear the message because they can't get past the way it was delivered. They get depressed instead of determined. They sulk, feel sorry for themselves, and choose, in that challenging moment, to step out of the arena and become the victim. Not only do losers miss out on a chance to get better, they also make a sorry statement to their coach about their low level of toughness and trust.

Getting coached isn't easy, but like any Hidden Talent area, the more you do it the better you get. As you make winning choices, you develop winning habits and start to create your identity as someone who wants to get better, who's humble enough to get coached, and who's determined to use every opportunity as a chance to prove it.

Getting Coached – Separation

As we continue to climb the ladder and strive for more in any important area of life, new opportunities present themselves. We get to play on a bigger stage with brighter lights. We get to experience new levels of success. We get more recognition for our winning performance. But climbing the ladder also brings with it new challenges. There are more eyes on you than ever before. There's a higher standard of performance up here than there was down below. There's a new level of competition you haven't seen. In some ways, the better you get, the tougher it gets.

The same can be said for getting coached. The better you get, the better your coaching will get. At the same time, the better you get, the tougher your coaching will get. The higher up the ladder you climb, the more there is at stake. Your boss there will have a more challenging expectation for your performance than what you've had before. So if you're really after something big and important, who will you have prepared yourself to be, and how will you have prepared yourself to handle the coaching that's to come when you get there?

Those who can't get coached today will likely be unprepared to get coached on a bigger stage tomorrow. Maybe you've always relied on your natural, surface-level talent to carry you. For people with that kind of talent, it can be easy to argue that you don't need coaching. But by justifying that you can do it yourself, you've closed yourself off to listening, learning, and improving.

If you've humbly accepted that being your best will require more than just your natural, surface-level ability, then you've probably come to recognize and then work to develop this Hidden Talent. As you climb the ladder and face the new level of competition that's waiting there, you'll be prepared to handle the tough coaching that's to come. Consider how this might separate you from others who are still trying to rely on talent that's no longer sufficient.

Keep climbing that ladder. See all the opportunities that the next level can present, but recognize too the challenges that will accompany it. If you're doing something big and important, there should be something at stake. There should be a boss with a high expectation, and there should be some pressure, some excitement, and some competitiveness existing there. If none of those things exist – if there's nothing at stake, there's no expectation, and there's no pressure, excitement, or competitiveness? Then how big and important could it be?

I hope you see that the habits you're building today will determine how prepared you are to handle that type of environment. Losers today are training themselves to be losers tomorrow. They're the ones who'll feel victimized or picked on by the person in charge. They'll trudge through their days, sulking around and feeling sorry for themselves. They won't thrive, they'll just try to survive, or they'll bail on their challenging situation and choose instead to play the victim. They'll quit and go find someplace with a lower expectation. Someplace with less at stake that doesn't require their very best.

Or, of course, you can train yourself today to be a champion. As you climb the ladder, you'll find bosses who are hard on you. You'll also find that you can handle it. Instead of feeling like someone's out to get you, you'll be more capable of seeing that maybe they just have a high expectation for your performance, and that with all there is at stake, you need to step up your game, get determined, and perform. There will be a lot on the line. Instead of being crippled by that fact, you'll be empowered by it.

Those who can get coached set themselves apart. By cultivating this talent, you create new opportunities to learn and improve. You also prove yourself trustworthy in the eyes of your coach, and reap the rewards that come with it. Your coach, along with many others, will play an important role in helping you become your very best. Remember, no one gets there alone.

KEY CONCEPTS FOR
GETTING COACHED

- Wherever it is you dream about going, and whoever it is you envision yourself being when you arrive at your destination, the truth is you cannot get there alone.

- Getting coached is a lot less about who your coach is and a lot more about who you are and what you're after.

- Whether he loves the role he's been given or not, the champion has chosen to step into the arena and be a star in that role.

- The champion knows that proving he can be trusted in his current role is the best way to prove he's ready for a bigger role.

- Those who've developed their discipline actually end up finding more responsibility, more opportunity, and more freedom than those who haven't.

WHAT CHAMPIONS SAY ABOUT
GETTING COACHED

"Everyone needs a coach. It doesn't matter if you're a basketball player, a tennis player, a gymnast, or a bridge player." *-Bill Gates*

"I love being coached. I get angry when I'm not coached. I ask a lot of questions and certainly appreciate any insight and feedback. I think if you ever stop listening to coaching or stop asking questions, you probably need to be doing something else." *-Peyton Manning*

"If you're not humble, it's hard to be coached. If you can't be coached, it's hard to get better." *-Jay Wright*

"You should always want your coach to be critical. It gives you an opportunity to learn and to overcome adversity." *-Steve Nash*

"The fact of the matter is, if you want to be good, you really don't have a lot of choices, because it takes what it takes.." *-Nick Saban*

CHAPTER 12:

BEING A
TEAMMATE

YOUR HIDDEN TALENT

Being a Teammate – Recognition

As we keep moving through the Hidden Talents, hopefully you continue to see how connected each is to all the rest. In the previous chapter, we talked about how developing your ability to get coached means recognizing that you can't be your best without help. The same is true for your experience as a teammate. No matter how much talent you have on the surface, if you don't dig deep enough to recognize the important role your teammates will play in your pursuit of excellence – and the important role you'll play in theirs – then you'll never reach your potential. That's because champions don't just win; they help those around them win, too.

The foundation of being a teammate is built on a sense of selflessness and sacrifice. Champions recognize that when they give up some of what's theirs for the good of the team – some of their stats, some of their glory, some of their ego – then what's theirs has a way of coming back to them, and then some. Excellence requires a sense of selflessness and sacrifice, and contrary to what our culture would have you believe, success honors that sense. Champions recognize that holding tightly to what's yours instead of sharing it with others actually means very little if it stands in the way of winning. You can have all the stats, all the glory, and all the ego in the world. People can heap praise on your individual performance, and that performance can be impressive by itself, but as a champion, you're driven by something bigger: your team's success.

That's why winning teams get assists. Assists are a statistical number kept in sports like basketball or soccer where credit's given not only to the person who scored, but also to the person who gave up their chance to score and instead made the pass — or the assist — that led to their teammate's success. If you dig deep into any championship team or organization, you'll find that assists, in all their many forms, are an integral part of the culture and a regular practice among its members.

On great teams, you'll find team members who are willingly and selflessly choosing to sacrifice something of their own in order to help a teammate succeed. They are intentionally and mindfully choosing others over themselves. Champions recognize that they *can* set someone else up for success, but more importantly, they recognize that in order to become their best and help their team become its best, they *must*. They value assists in themselves and in each other.

It's worth stopping to consider what assists look like for your team and who it is that's doing this important, yet often unnoticed work. If you're part of a successful organization, then you're probably scoring plenty of points, either literally for figuratively, and those who are scoring those points are probably getting plenty of attention. Their role in winning is easy to see. But who are the champions on your team that are willingly and selflessly choosing to sacrifice something of their own in order to help their teammates succeed and help their team win? Those are champion teammates.

Champions recognize the important role those sacrifices play in a winning organization. If you're a champion yourself, then you're responsible for recognizing who it is that's chosen to sacrifice for the good of your group. You're responsible for acknowledging those people and their important, yet often unnoticed work. You should also be able to identify ways that you're doing your part to get some assists. Even if you're the one scoring many of the points, there are still plenty of sacrifices you can make.

How are you willingly and selflessly choosing to give up something of your own in order to help a teammate succeed or help your team win? How are you adding to the winning culture of your organization by setting someone else up for success? And lastly, do you recognize how important that work is? Even if no one else does, you need to recognize the role it plays in helping your team becomes its best and in helping you become a champion.

Being a Teammate – Development

Once you recognize the important place being a teammate has in your pursuit of excellence, it's time to get to work developing this Hidden Talent. As always, the work it takes to develop yourself as a teammate isn't easy. In today's world, we're conditioned to make it all about us. Willingly and selflessly choosing to sacrifice something of our own for someone else is a challenging arena to step into. The opponent there is our own selfishness – our stats, our glory, our ego. Fighting the urge to make it all about us, and instead choosing to support, uplift, and empower those on our team takes trust and strength and confidence. But as always, the more you fight to become a champion in this area, the more you recognize its importance, and the stronger and better at it you become.

There are plenty of ways you can be a great teammate and assist others, regardless of the role you play on your team. Sometimes those choices you make – to inconvenience yourself, to sacrifice something for someone else or to willingly shoulder a burden – will get the recognition they deserve. Often, though, choosing to step into the arena and be a great teammate goes unrecognized and unacknowledged. The shot makers and point scorers will probably get all the attention while your important contribution may get overlooked. But just because doing the right thing doesn't get noticed doesn't mean it shouldn't be done.

One simple way you can develop yourself as a teammate is by increasing the burden you're capable of bearing for others. Accepting blame means bearing the heavy load that comes with taking responsibility for some kind of failure or fault. When things go wrong – especially when there's a lot on the line – nobody likes taking the blame, because it shines a light on our shortcomings.

Sometimes, of course, it's obvious who's to blame. But when it's not obvious, there's a unique arena created. In moments like those, you'll see the losers step back. They aren't strong or confident enough to step into that arena. They're selfish and needy. Their identities are fragile. Losers usually need to blame someone else for what went wrong before they can ever think about moving on. Adversity like this keeps them from playing in the present.

Champions recognize this moment as a chance to step forward and get an assist. They're strong and confident enough to willingly shoulder this burden for their weaker, less confident teammates. When things go wrong, champions accept the blame they're due. And because they recognize how hard it is for the losers to step into the arena and carry that burden themselves, champions also sometimes choose to selflessly shoulder the burden for their less capable and more fragile teammates, even if the blame may not necessarily belong to them. Why would the champion do such a thing? Because champions win.

As a champion, you know you'll need everyone's best effort to win the game you find yourself in. You also know that your weaker, less capable teammates may be crippled by an accusation of blame and may carry that burden with them, for who knows how long. So as a champion, you may choose to take it on yourself, own it, and then leave it behind so your team can move on toward your bigger objective – victory. Is choosing to step up and shoulder that burden convenient? No. Is it fair? Probably not. But is it evidence of your strength, your selflessness, and your commitment to being a teammate? Absolutely.

You've chosen to step into the arena with your teammate in mind. In a situation like this, there's a lot here you can't control. You can't control the mistake that was made. You can't control your teammate's mediocre response to it. You can't control how others viewed the mistake or judged who was responsible. All you can control in that moment is your belief that a focus on winning the game is way more important than a focus on pointing the finger. So you take the bullet, because you've developed the toughness to handle this adversity. You are strong and confident, and you can take it.

Now, do you need to take the bullet every time? No. There may be times when it's necessary for you to step up and dispute someone's accusation of blame. Other times, you might be outside a dispute and need to support someone else who's responsible. You don't need to take all the blame all the time. But if you're strong and confident enough to accept the blame that's rightfully yours, and occasionally capable of stepping up and accepting some that may not be? Then you're a teammate who'll bring value to those around you. And if you can't take any of the blame, any of the time? Then you're mentally weak, fragile, and insecure. And in that case, you can kiss your champion self goodbye.

Great teams are made up of great teammates. Consider what a team of strong, secure, champion-minded teammates could do if they were constantly stepping into the arena with their teammates in mind. If they were looking for opportunities to willingly shoulder one another's burdens instead of weakly and gutlessly avoiding responsibility. That's a group of individuals who makes one another better. That's a group that wins.

Just as champion teammates assist one another by bearing more of the burden, they also do it by giving away more of the glory. When things go well there's recognition, and recognition feels good. So when someone praises you for your accomplishment, what is your response? This is another arena that as a champion teammate, you can choose to step into. Like always, being a teammate involves giving up something of your own to benefit someone else. Are you willing to make that winning choice? That's the kind of decision that separates the champion from the loser. We said it already – losers are selfish and needy. Because their identities are fragile, they have a hard time giving the credit away.

Champions, on the other hand, recognize that if being a teammate is built on a foundation of selflessness, nothing is more selfless than saying, "Thanks for the acknowledgement, but the credit actually belongs to him over there." Think about the impact you can have on your teammates if you chose to give them some of the glory for your success. In all honesty, if you're the reason your team's won, you can trust that people will see it. You don't have to worry about your contributions being overlooked. Deservingly, the credit might belong to you. But even then – *especially then* – if you're willing to pass the praise on to others? Then you're taking what's yours and using it to make everyone on your team bigger. And stronger. And better.

When you bring out the best in others, it has a way of bringing out the best in you. Remember, when it comes to chasing excellence, no one gets there alone. Empowering others invites them to join you in your pursuit. By sharing your success – by giving it away – you actually set yourself up for more success. On the other hand, when you work hard to hoard all the acknowledgement, it turns you away from others and the opportunities they present to help you improve. That's why this commitment, to being a teammate, isn't just a crucial part of helping your group become its best. It's crucial to you becoming your best, too.

Being a Teammate – Separation

No matter who you are or what role you play on your team, becoming an elite teammate will set you apart. When you're committed to bringing out the best in others, you stand out from the crowd. Your impact can be seen and felt by everyone around you.

Maybe you are the star of the show. If so, you have an important responsibility to those on your team. You'll always be getting plenty of attention, plenty of press, and plenty of glory. Those are the perks of being the best. But without a commitment to doing those things that great teammates do – things like accepting blame and deflecting credit – all those perks can easily create a sense of entitlement in the star. If he gets all the glory while scowling down on every mistake his less talented teammates make, he becomes what many stars become to their team: an easy guy to resent.

In any area of life, it's not easy to help someone you resent. It definitely becomes more obligation than opportunity. In fact, it might be nice to see the superstar you resent fail every now and then. If you're a superstar who's serious about becoming your best, then you have to see clearly the important role your teammates will play in helping you get there. You need them to do more than just tolerate your success. You need them to support it.

When you commit to being a teammate, you become more than just your average superstar. You earn your teammate's respect, not their resentment. You become someone they *want* to support, someone they *want* to help, someone they *want* to cheer for. Instead of secretly hoping you fail, they'll be openly looking for ways to help you succeed. Especially if they know you're willing to share the attention, the press, and the glory, they'll go out of their way to assist you. As the star, you set the example for what a teammate should look like in your organization. How you choose to handle your responsibility as a teammate filters down to everyone else. By doing it right and doing it well, you set yourself and your team apart.

Okay, you might be thinking, but what if I'm not the star? Can being a teammate help separate me if I'm just another average member of my team? Does it matter for me, too? Absolutely it does. Role players don't usually get much credit, but the truth is they often play a critical role in a team's success. And even though you may not see it in the box score or mentioned in the paper, your commitment to keeping your team connected is a unique ability that can set you apart, even if you aren't the star. These guys – the ones intentionally and mindfully bonding the team together – are known as the "glue guys," and every team chasing excellence needs them.

Your Hidden Talent is of course the main ingredient in this glue. Some jobs on a team only the superstar can take on, but the beauty of this role is that anyone who's willing can accept it. *You* can accept it. It may not come with much credit from the outside, but the more glue you apply and the more you bring your team together, the more important you become. Your dedication to excellence in this area increases your value.

As a glue guy, that value lies in having made yourself a vital part of your teammates' success story. That's your goal, to become a part of your team's winning formula. Become someone your teammates love playing with and don't want to play without. Your teammates need to recognize that this place would be worse off without you here. They need to think, "He's the guy who's willing to do the dirty work so that I can get all the glory. He's the guy who's happiest when I have success. He cares most about winning, which is what I care about. I don't always know how, but he just makes me better." By willingly and intentionally choosing to make other people important, you help make yourself important, too.

When the team succeeds, the superstar gets the attention, the press, and the glory. Their obvious, surface-level talent makes them valuable. But if you're a role player, you don't have that same luxury. You're responsible for finding some other way to contribute, to make yourself valuable, and to set yourself apart. When you become a glue guy – someone who willingly gives up some of himself to help bring his team together, someone who becomes a part of his teammate's winning formula, someone who helps his team bond together and keep connected – you make yourself a valuable member of your team. Like many of the choices you make as a teammate, on the surface your work may go unnoticed. But for those who dig deeper into the group's success, they might find you've become your team's most valuable player.

KEY CONCEPTS FOR
BEING A TEAMMATE

- On great teams, you'll find team members who are willingly and selflessly choosing to sacrifice something of their own in order to help a teammate succeed.

- Often, choosing to step into the arena and be a great teammate goes unrecognized and unacknowledged. But just because doing the right thing doesn't get noticed doesn't mean it shouldn't be done.

- Just as champion teammates assist one another by bearing more of the burden, they also do it by giving away more of the glory.

- By sharing your success – by giving it away – you actually set yourself up for more success.

- When you're committed to bringing out the best in others, you stand out from the crowd.

WHAT CHAMPIONS SAY ABOUT
BEING A TEAMMATE

"The best compliment I can give a player is that he's the best teammate." *-Terry Francona*

"The strength of the team is each individual member. The strength of each member is the team." *-Phil Jackson*

"The way a team plays as a whole determines its success. You may have the greatest bunch of individual stars in the world, but if they don't play together, the club won't be worth a dime."
-Babe Ruth

"Five guys on the court working together can achieve more than five talented individuals who come and go as individuals." *-Kareem Abdul-Jabbar*

"If anything goes bad, I did it. If anything goes semi-good, we did it. If anything goes really good, then you did it." *-Bear Bryant*

CHAPTER 13:

TAKING RISKS

YOUR HIDDEN TALENT

Taking Risks – Recognition

From right where you are here near the end of the book, stop and think back to Teddy Roosevelt's description of the champion – the man in the arena we described back in Chapter 1. Now take a minute and paint a more personal picture of that man or woman. Make it more than just some person. Make it you. And don't make it some symbolic arena. Make it your arena. Create that image in your mind. See yourself standing there in the shadows of your arena's entryway. The bleachers are vast, but empty; it's deathly quiet. What's the battle, the competition, the enemy look like there in front of you? What adversary do you see waiting for you there in the middle of the arena?

This is the moment of truth – your moment of choice. With the bleachers empty, you could easily step farther back into the shadows and exit quietly out the back without anyone ever knowing. The loser in you might encourage it, in fact. You deserve a break. You're tired and a little beat up. Your face still shows evidence of the dust and sweat and blood from yesterday's fight, and today's enemy – who's entered the stadium and now stands in the center of that open space – is staring you down and snarling there before you. He appears even bigger and meaner than the foe you faced yesterday. Yes, you could turn and walk away, but that's not you. Instead, you take in a deep breath, and as you exhale your eyes narrow, your jaw clenches, and your foot moves forward across that line, out of the shadow and into the light. You're not running. Instead, you've chosen to step in. You're ready to fight, and win…again.

That winning choice you've made – to step into the arena – is a risk, for sure. Winning's only possible for those with the courage it takes to step in, but as we've said already, stepping in doesn't guarantee winning, at least not on the scoreboard. As Roosevelt said, champions err. They fall short. Sometimes they lose. Hopefully you've come to recognize, however, that winning is about more than just a number on a scoreboard. For champions, winning is really about choosing today to cast another vote for your champion self. It's about your willingness to do what champions do. As you make that choice, day after day, and continue to develop, you find that the number on the scoreboard usually takes care of itself.

Taking a risk in any area of life involves going somewhere unknown. What you'll find when you get to your destination is unclear; that's why it's a risk. You might find victory, success, happiness…or you might find failure, loss, and pain. The questions that exist at the root of risk are always the same. What will be the result when I get there? Will it be worth it? What if it fails and I look like a loser and an idiot?

What if I get there and realize it's not what I thought, and that I've wasted my time?

These are questions each of us has to answer every time we stand there in the entryway of our arena. When you boil it all down, what we choose in that moment – to give into our fear or to follow our faith – that's what determines our destiny. There's no way to know for sure what today's competition might bring, but champions have decided that the pursuit of greatness is worth the possibility of failure, and that taking risks will always be a part of life if we really choose to live it.

It is worth clarifying that champions also recognize the difference between good risk and bad risk. To simply say, "Champions take risks, period" is not true, and really just plain dumb. Taking a good risk means recognizing that what you're after is worth the sacrifice that's required. Bad risk simply means what you're after isn't worth the price you'd have to pay. Recognition in this Hidden Talent area requires discernment. Champions aren't blindly and ignorantly taking stupid chances. They're aware, insightful, and ready to seize the right opportunities – the ones that lead to greatness.

Being your best requires the ability to recognize those opportunities when they're presented. You'll have your chances, but most of them will be available only for a limited time, and once they're gone, they'll be gone for good. As the old saying goes, "You can't be afraid to go out on a limb; that's where the fruit is." That's true for each of us, in whatever areas we are chasing excellence. Your opportunities are out there, but probably not for long. You've got to have your radar up. Be ready to spot your chance, and when you do, know that it's probably short-lived.

If what you're doing is big and important, then fear will probably be a part of the experience. After all, that limb's flimsy…and if it breaks? It looks like a long way down. Being a champion doesn't mean you aren't ever afraid, but it does mean you've clarified for yourself the truth about fear: that the worry we create in our minds is often an illusion. The truth is that fear is strong, but that faith and hope and love are actually stronger. And champions recognize that they aren't defined by their fear. They're defined by their triumph over fear. So while the losers are fearfully clinging to the trunk of the tree, champions are out there on the limb, going to get what they want.

It's worth considering, when your opportunity comes, what it is you've prepared yourself to do, and who it is you've prepared yourself to be.

Taking Risks - Development

Like it does for each one, developing this Hidden Talent starts with a choice. Once you've recognized the opportunity in front of you, choosing to go out on a limb and take that risk starts the growth process. Each time you boldly make that winning choice, your talent develops. Your courage grows and your fear diminishes. The better you get, the easier and more habitual that choice becomes, and the more votes you cast for your champion self. So how do you start developing this talent in your world today? Where exactly do you start?

You can start by simply changing the way you approach today's competition. Instead of just going through the motions – instead of just kind of, sort of hoping you win – intentionally and mindfully choose to really, truly compete. We're talking an "all in" commitment to winning, wherever where you are and whatever you're doing today.

The truth is, really, truly competing like that is a risk. We talked about it back in the introduction and we've touched on it throughout the book, that in many ways life is a game to be won or lost today. Anywhere responsibility or opportunity exists in life, competition exists, too. It might involve the challenge of competing against someone or something else. More often and more importantly, it's the challenge you're facing against yourself and the best you're capable of. Champions recognize that there's a game being played. They recognize how winning is really defined and what exactly it takes to win. And no matter how big or how small the contest, they're "all in" on their commitment to competing.

Really, truly competing means giving *everything* you've got. It means putting your very best on the line and pushing all your chips to the middle of the table. For the loser, driven by that fear of failure or of looking bad, really, truly competing like that usually isn't worth the risk. But the fact is, sometimes competing isn't pretty. You'll be scraping and clawing. You'll be dusty, sweaty, and bloody. And if you're more concerned with your image than you are with doing whatever it takes to win, then competing probably isn't worth the risk, and winning probably isn't in your future.

Beyond that, losers recognize that going "all in" can leave you exposed there in the face of your failure. It's easier to avoid that risk and construct a safety net for yourself in case you come up short. "I didn't really give it my all," the loser contends. "If I would've, I probably would've won." By holding back – even a little – he creates a built-in excuse for losing.

Overcoming those fears and the sorry excuses that come with them isn't easy. Really, truly competing *is* a risk...for anyone. If you go "all in," and lose, it means your best wasn't good enough, plain and simple, and that can be a tough pill to swallow. But it's worth considering the different ways there are to lose in this world. Some of them we can be proud of, and some we'll regret.

I don't know what your competition looks like today, but I do know there's an arena for you to step into, and an opponent waiting there. It's possible the game you're playing today no one else will ever witness. The arena is empty, save for you and your opponent. In your moment of decision, there in the entryway, you could probably retreat further into the shadows and avoid today's fight altogether. It's likely no one else will ever know.

You could step timidly forward, armed with your fears and excuses, and willing to accept mediocrity. Or you could put your very best on the line, push all your chips to the middle of the table, and go "all in" to win. How you decide to approach this private, personal battle today is up to you. But even if no one else knows, you'll know, today, either the pride of a battle well fought, or the regret of a missed opportunity. And you'll be preparing yourself, one way or another, for the bigger battles that are to come.

Someday soon you'll probably find yourself in the entryway of your biggest, most public battle yet. Picture that scene. Now the arena's packed – it's standing room only. Waiting there in the shadows, you can literally feel the electrifying buzz of the crowd. This place is rocking. The hair on the back of your neck stands on end as you look out on your opponent, waiting there in the light. There's no retreating today, no avoiding this, your most public battle yet. But while you'll have to step forward in that moment, you will still have a choice. You know the fruit you're after sits on a flimsy, wobbling branch that can only be reached by giving everything you've got. The crowd erupts – a deafening roar – as you step out of the shadows and into the light. The game is on. Which "you" has shown up?

You can act like you're really striving, give something resembling your best, come up short and accept that it just wasn't meant to be. Or you can stretch, and fight, and probably look awkward or goofy or silly there relentlessly pursuing your dream out on the limb, all while dangling over the failure waiting to clobber you down below. And in the face of all of it – your fear, your excuses, your critics there watching – you can go "all in" to win the prize. You can do a lot of things there in your moment of opportunity, but here's one thing you can't do: you can't rise to the occasion. You can only perform at the level to which you've been trained.

That means if you want to develop your Hidden Talent, if you want to cultivate your courage, and if you want to seize the opportunities required for you to be your best on your big day, then you've got to get busy competing at your highest level on this day. No matter how big or small today's arena, no

169

matter how public or private today's fight, no matter how loud or how quiet the voice of your fear, today you must choose to really, truly compete. Put your very best on the line. Push your chips to the middle of the table, and go "all in." You'll be glad you did.

Taking Risks – Separation

Conduct a Google search for "the elderly's biggest regrets," and you'll find a number of interesting results. Some are scientific studies, others personal stories, but all of them serve as sobering reflections on life as it nears its conclusion. The similarity of responses is striking, and each one of them offers us some powerful advice for living a life we can be proud of, here while we're still creating it. Among those most popular responses was simply, "I wish I would have taken more risks." Sadly, it appears that for many people, failing to develop this Hidden Talent kept them, in their own minds, from living their best lives.

It's safe to say, then, that developing the foresight and the courage needed to take risks is an integral part of *you* living *your* best life. By recognizing the important role that "Taking Risks" plays in becoming a champion, and then by choosing to step into that arena and do the work it takes to develop that ability each day, you set yourself apart from so many people who, sadly, may end up looking back on their lives with regret.

This chapter clarifies, as much as any other, that champions aren't who they are because they win. Champions are who they are because they've developed, among other things, the courage it takes to go for it, to get in the arena and really, truly compete. It doesn't guarantee winning, but it does put them in the best position to win. More importantly – win or lose – it promises a performance they can be proud of, and one they won't look back on with regret.

Losers, we've proven throughout the book, aren't who they are because they lose, either. It's how they play, how they fight, how they compete that makes them who they are. Fear dictates their thoughts, choices, and actions. It's what motivates and drives their performance, and what ultimately keeps them from going "all in." Of course they may stumble into winning once in a while, but even in winning, losers know deep down they left something on the table. Regardless of the outcome, they'll probably look back at some point and painfully have to admit they could've done better.

The truth is, regret stinks. Nobody is undefeated in their fight against regret – we all have some. If we could build a time machine and go back for at least a few do-overs in life, most of us probably would. Unfortunately, that's not how it works. There is something we can do, though, and that's learn from the regrettable mistakes we've made in our past. We can also learn from the mistakes of those who've been someplace we haven't yet been – but someplace we're all headed – like so many of the elderly who struggle with risk and regret as their lives comes to a close. We can use those lessons to help us make winning choices about how we compete today, and in doing so start the process of building better identities for ourselves – ones we can be proud of for life.

Every day you commit to that process, you separate yourself from those around you. You make yourself more aware of your opportunities, and you develop the courage required to seize them. As your talent develops, you may find it's hard *not* to stand out. In a world full of people stepping farther back into the shadows, those boldly stepping forward into the light are increasingly rare. Real competitors have become harder and harder to find, and those who live life out on the limb have become even more uncommon. If you dare to venture out there – despite your fear – there's a lot you'll find. Opportunity. Success. Failure. Who knows. But there are also a few things you won't find out there. Most importantly among them, you won't find regret.

KEY CONCEPTS FOR
TAKING RISKS

- There's no way to know for sure what today's competition might bring, but champions have decided that the pursuit of greatness is worth the possibility of failure, and that taking risks will always be a part of life if we choose to live it.

- Really, truly competing is a risk. It means giving *everything* you've got. It means putting your very best on the line and pushing all your chips to the middle of the table.

- It's worth considering the different ways there are to lose in this world. Some of them we can be proud of, and some we'll regret.

- Even if no one else knows, you'll know, today, either the pride of a battle well fought or the regret of a missed opportunity.

- If you want to develop your Hidden Talent, if you want to cultivate your courage, and if you want to seize the opportunities required for you to be your best on your big day, you've got to get busy competing on this day.

WHAT CHAMPIONS SAY ABOUT
TAKING RISKS

"You miss 100% of the shots you don't take."
-Wayne Gretzky

"Life is not a spectator sport. If you're going to spend your whole life in the grandstands just watching what goes on, in my opinion you're wasting your life." *-Jackie Robinson*

"Only those who dare to fail greatly can ever achieve greatly." *-Robert F. Kennedy*

"Show me the guy who's afraid to look bad, and I'll show you the guy you can beat every time."
-Lou Brock

"There is no passion to be found in playing small - in settling for a life that is less than the one you are capable of living." *-Nelson Mandela*

CHAPTER 14:

CHOOSING A POSITIVE ATTITUDE

YOUR HIDDEN TALENT

Choosing a Positive Attitude – Recognition

By now, I hope your time here has given you a chance to recognize all that a commitment to cultivating your Hidden Talent requires, but more importantly, all it provides. The more you embrace the process of learning, growing, and developing each day, the more your talent separates you, not only from those you're competing with and against, but from that old, mediocre version of yourself, too. Your Hidden Talent grants you access to opportunities you wouldn't otherwise be afforded, and it supplies more pride for what you accomplish in life and less regret over what you didn't.

Those are all big-picture benefits, what you reap in the long term by sowing in the here and now. But that commitment to cultivating your Hidden Talent provides a few important things you can use for today, too. First, it provides you with a purpose. It helps you recognize that today matters. Wherever you are and whatever you're doing, there's an important reason why you're here. Even if the work itself doesn't seem that meaningful on the surface, when you dig deeper you recognize that how you approach this work actually really matters. Why? Because how you do anything is how you do everything. This thing you're doing – right here, right now – is another opportunity to train, and prepare, and cast another vote for your best self.

Second, that commitment to cultivating your Hidden Talent provides you with a vision. By recognizing who it is you can become and what exactly you're capable of in these important areas, you create a clearer picture of the champion self you're working to develop. As a champion, you recognize that the best is yet to come for you, that you've got plenty more to do and achieve, and that you're excited and hopeful for the future you recognize you have the chance to create. Together, a mighty purpose for today and a clear vision for tomorrow come together to produce this last Hidden Talent: a positive attitude.

Negativity is a real threat to any person or organization's pursuit of excellence. Consider what it is that often brings that negativity to the surface. If you've ever struggled with feeling negative, what's brought it out in you? A lack of purpose might be the culprit, the feeling that what you're doing doesn't matter. The truth is, it's usually not the hard work that burns us out; it's the meaningless work. When we lose touch with our purpose, negativity can easily creep in. A lack of vision could also have been the problem. If you're hopeless about the future – if you think your best days are behind you and you've got nothing more to work for or accomplish, then of course you're more likely to turn negative. Purpose and vision help each of us stay positive.

Choosing a positive attitude means choosing to see things clearly every day. It means recognizing what really matters, what really defines winning, and what really makes a champion a champion. A positive attitude is the by-product of doing what champions do – of chasing excellence, of making winning choices, and of cultivating your Hidden Talent. It springs naturally from intentionally igniting your passion and developing a new ceiling for your effort. It comes from elevating your levels of personal responsibility and accountability. From developing your toughness and building your courage. It's cultivated by a hunger to improve, a growing sense of discipline and trustworthiness, and a focus on service and selflessness. Your positive attitude is the result of your vision – who you've recognized you can become – and your purpose – the important work you're doing today to get there.

Losers don't see things the same way. They aren't chasing excellence or making winning choices. They don't recognize the gifts they've been given and aren't committed to the work it takes to turn them from potential to reality. Instead, they usually focus on the unfairness of their circumstances, on protecting their image, or on avoiding the fight that comes with stepping into the arena. The result? Circumstantial effort and lack of accountability. Complaining or blaming someone or something for what's hard. A lack of discipline and trustworthiness. And of course, a negative attitude. It's all a by-product of their focus and their perspective.

The writer and philosopher Henry David Thoreau said, "It's not what you look at that matters, it's what you see." That's so true; there's great power in our perspective. Isn't it funny how two people can look at the same thing and see something entirely different? That's one way people describe the difference between optimists (those who see the glass half-full) and pessimists (who see it half-empty). It's a great way to describe the difference between champions and losers, too. Both are looking at the experiences, opportunities, and challenges that come with pursuing excellence. One sees them positively and the other negatively. It's worth a minute to consider…how do you see them?

Of course, we all wish that today could be a glass-totally-full day, where everything goes just the way we want. Unfortunately, most days don't follow that script. But champions recognize that the hand they've been dealt today isn't nearly as important as how they play that hand. Because they're focused on the process, they see that even with less than ideal circumstances, they can use today as an opportunity to step into the arena and get better.

That's the purpose that today provides. For champions, just because conditions aren't perfect doesn't mean they can't choose a positive attitude. As we've said already, champions recognize that challenge and adversity are a part of their story. They recognize that our circumstances only have power if we choose to give them power, and that how we respond to that challenge and adversity is what really matters.

By seeing the big picture, champions recognize that today's result doesn't define them; it's how they've chosen to compete today that defines them. They've experienced plenty of challenging days before now and they know they've got plenty more to come. Tomorrow will be a new day – if they're lucky, maybe a glass-totally-full day. But no matter what, embracing the process allows them to make the most of what's available. They're busy using today to get better. They've clarified a vision for who they're working to become and a purpose for why there here, and it's that vision and purpose that create a positive attitude in spite of the struggle.

Choosing a Positive Attitude – Development

Choosing a positive attitude simply means seeing, thinking, and acting in a way that moves you in a positive direction – it means living with purpose toward the vision you have for what's possible. Being positive can have a negative connotation when it's misdefined as some naïve ignorance of reality or intentionally burying your head in the sand to avoid the truth. That's not what we're talking about here.

Instead, being positive means looking reality and the truth that accompanies it in the eye. It means stepping up and fighting to become the best version of yourself because you see that *that* work can't afford to go *undone*. It means doing what it takes to turn your potential into reality. It means really competing to win today – getting dusty and sweaty and bloody – and loving every minute of it. A positive attitude is a productive attitude. It's a progressive attitude. It's a purposeful attitude.

If you want to take the "glass half-full/glass half-empty" analogy a little farther, think of it this way. If the water in your glass represents the situations and circumstances of life today, then the seed buried in the pot next to it represents your potential. You recognize that you've been given this seed as a gift and charged with the responsibility of cultivating it. You are responsible for deciding what it becomes.

Each day your glass of water gets filled. Some days are awesome, easy, and successful – your glass gets filled to the top. Other days are harder and more challenging – your glass gets filled only a little. And while your loser self wants to dwell on how much water did or didn't get put in the glass, your champion self chooses to focus on a different question: what am I going to do with what I've been given? When you choose to use today to get better, and to move yourself toward the vision you've created, then your positive attitude will naturally reflect your productive, progressive, purposeful work. This is development.

Sure, like everyone you would prefer that every glass you got was filled to the brim, but you'll gladly take and use whatever's available. You've intentionally, mindfully, and exceptionally chosen to develop your champion self. No matter how much water you did or didn't get, it's useful to growing that seed of potential. You know that growth only happens one way – the long, slow way, one tiny speck at a time. You also know that seed's getting stronger, that its roots are growing deeper, and that today it's bigger and better than it was yesterday. You have a clear picture of what it can become, and you're excited to get back to work using whatever happens to help it improve again tomorrow.

Of course, looking reality and the truth that accompanies it in the eye means acknowledging that being positive isn't always easy. There will be negativity to deal with, maybe sometimes even from the loser inside your own head. You may have to fight sometimes to stay connected to your purpose. Remember that even if what you're doing doesn't seem that important, how you choose to do it is. You may also have to fight from time to time to stay connected to your vision. Don't lose sight of what's possible as long as you're committed to the process it takes to get there.

More likely, as a champion, you'll have to step up and fight the negativity that comes from those around you. There will be plenty of people who don't have the same purpose or vision you do, and some of them may be playing an important role in the story you're trying to write. Maybe it's a teammate, a co-worker, a coach, or a boss. It could be a family member or a friend, even a complete stranger who's chosen to bring their negativity into your world. You'll have to deal with cynicism, criticism, and pessimism. People around you will be easily angered and easily discouraged. Some may be jealous; others may just be hopeless. It may feel at times like your purpose and your vision are being bombarded at every turn.

But as always, as a champion, you are defined by your willingness to step into the arena and fight. In this specific area of your life, that means fighting to remain your most productive, most progressive, and most positive self. Your purpose for today and your vision for tomorrow – and the attitude they produce – must be bigger and more powerful than all that negativity around you. The more you fight for what you know is important, the more you develop this Hidden Talent. And the more you develop, the more unique you become.

Choosing a Positive Attitude – Separation

Doing the hard work it takes to intentionally develop a positive attitude creates something inside that every champion possesses, something that sets him or her apart. It creates hope. Without a clear purpose for today or a clear vision for tomorrow, hope can be hard to come by. With that purpose and vision, it's hard *not* to come by. Hope is a powerful thing – in fact, it's a competitive advantage for champions. It breeds real confidence that sets them apart. It's another thing that separates the very best from everyone else.

Hope alone isn't enough, of course. Champions don't just sit around painting a pretty picture in their minds; they get busy doing the tough, important work required to make their dream come true. By combining those two elements – real, authentic hope *and* a willingness to work – you can rise up to meet any challenge, overcome any adversity, and embrace any struggle that comes with pursuing excellence. Hope simply won't allow you to quit, even when the critics say you should probably just give up, throw in the towel, and walk away.

For the loser, hope is fragile and easily extinguished. While the champion says, "It may be difficult, but it is possible," the loser says, "It may be possible, but it's too difficult." It's amazing, really, how quickly and easily the loser can accept defeat. The truth is, often when we find ourselves struggling, trailing, or facing defeat, there may still be enough time to come back and win, if we'd just keep competing until it's over. Sadly, though, for most people, a few challenging circumstances eliminate whatever chance of winning still exists. "Why even try?" seems to be the loser's response to this adversity. For anyone who really wants to win, the answer to that question seems obvious: because trying, as hard as you can for as long as possible, keeps whatever small chance you have of winning alive!

By developing your positive attitude, you not only build your capacity for hope, you also build your confidence. Again, not because you're naively assuming that today's gonna be easy. Actually, it's just the opposite. You're confident because you know you can handle whatever's coming today – even what's not easy. You're not stepping in the arena having created some picture of perfection. You know in reality your performance probably won't be perfect, but even so, you're confident because you know you can handle whatever you find.

If you make every play, come through in the clutch, and finish the job successfully, then great. That's what you've come here hoping would happen. You can use it and move on. If you make a mistake, encounter some hardship, or even come up short today, then you're prepared for that as well. As a champion you know that's part of the risk you take by stepping into the arena. And beyond that, you can use it, too, to get better, and then move on just the same. The more you develop your purpose and your vision, the more confidence you build for handling any situation, and the less you're held hostage by outcomes or circumstances you didn't expect.

When you're hopeful and confident in the way that you play, work, and live, you naturally create an infectious, positive energy. This is another way champions separate themselves from everyone else: they are energy givers. They spread their optimism, their hope, and their confidence to the people around them. Champions bring out the best in others and inspire them to be better. It's yet another example of one Hidden Talent area (Having a Positive Attitude) affecting another (Being a Teammate). The truth is, our energy – positive or negative – is contagious. It's worth stopping to consider whether yours is worth catching.

Developing your positive attitude makes you unique because, unfortunately, negativity seems to be everywhere these days. And while the winning choice to develop this Hidden Talent is available to each one of us, it isn't free. We are required to step in the arena and fight for it. Unfortunately, many people have given up the fight. With no purpose or vision, their lack of hope and confidence has made them less an energy giver and more an energy drain, sucking the life and spirit out of those around them. I hope you can see that you don't have to accept your place among these masses of mediocrity. Those people have made their choice, and you are the one responsible for making yours. So don't settle. You were created for something bigger and better. You were made to be a champion.

KEY CONCEPTS FOR
CHOOSING A
POSITIVE ATTITUDE

- A positive attitude is the by-product of doing what champions do – of chasing excellence, of making winning choices, and of cultivating your Hidden Talent.

- Your positive attitude is the result of your vision – who you've recognized you can become – and your purpose – the important work you're doing today to get there.

- Your purpose for today and your vision for tomorrow – and the attitude they produce – must be bigger and more powerful than all the negativity around you.

- While the champion says, "It may be difficult, but it is possible," the loser says, "It may be possible, but it's too difficult."

- The truth is, our energy – positive or negative – is contagious. It's worth stopping to consider whether yours is worth catching.

WHAT CHAMPIONS SAY ABOUT
CHOOSING A
POSITIVE ATTITUDE

"The attitude with which we approach our situation can determine our success or failure." -*Peyton Manning*

"I'm a very positive thinker, and I think that is what helps me the most in difficult moments." -*Roger Federer*

"Attitude is a little thing that makes a big difference." -*Winston Churchill*

"A positive attitude causes a chain reaction of positive thoughts, events, and outcomes. It is a catalyst, and it sparks extraordinary results." -*Wade Boggs*

"Belief in yourself is what happens when you know you've done the things that entitle you to success." -*Pat Summitt*

CONCLUSION

Recognition, development, separation. That's the process required to turn your potential into reality, and the process you've started here with this book. It all starts with recognition, and that's really what our time together has been – a chance to recognize some important realities about who you are and what you're capable of. I hope you recognize that champions aren't who they are because they win, and you won't be a champion because you win, either, in whatever important areas of life you are competing today. Actually, it's just the opposite that's true. Champions win because of who they are, and if you are to win, too, you'll win for that same reason – because of who you've worked hard to become.

Hopefully you've been able to recognize what really makes a champion a champion. First, champions are defined by their chase for excellence. Success is important, of course, but for champions success is the by-product of a bigger purpose – the pursuit of their personal best. Champions are also defined by their winning choices. Over time, those choices become habits, and eventually those habits create a strong character, identity, and reputation. Finally, champions are defined by their Hidden Talent. The best of the best are set apart by the unique qualities and characteristics they share...

They love the game.
They give their best.
They overcome adversity.
They seek improvement.
They get coached.
They know how to be a teammate.
They take risks.
They choose a positive attitude.

I also hope you've been able to recognize that you have all you need to become a champion yourself. It's easy to think that champions have been blessed with something the rest of us haven't, but the truth is we've all been given these gifts. That means choosing to ignore them and leave them undeveloped also means accepting that you haven't done all you can to reach your potential. It means settling for less than your best.

Finally, as part of this recognition process, I hope you've had a chance to recognize the Hidden Talent areas where you're currently excelling, along with those where you need some work. Hopefully you can look at some of those areas with pride in knowing you've developed them in the way you play, work, and live. That should serve as encouragement for sustaining your performance moving forward.

At the same time, your time in this book may have revealed some deficiencies in your champion-mindedness. You may even feel a little embarrassed now that you recognize what you've been capable of becoming next to the underwhelming reality of who you actually are. That should serve as motivation for intentionally and purposely working to improve your performance moving forward.

That's a lot of valuable work you've done throughout this book just in the recognition phase, and that work is crucial to becoming your best because you can't move forward in the process without it. At the same time, recognition is just the easy first step. Anyone can read the book and recognize their potential. Now you've gotta get to work. You've got to take what you've learned and put it into practice. It's time to step into the arena.

The good news is you can get started wherever you are. Your work today might be meaningful and important. If it is, you'll probably be performing under the spotlight of the big stage, with plenty of people there to witness it. If that's you today, then with everyone watching, have the courage required to step into the arena and play like a champion. Do what champions do.

Maybe today, the work you have in front of you seems small, simple, or insignificant. Maybe you're working alone in the dark. If that's you today, then even with no one watching, have the discipline required to step into the arena and play like a champion. Nobody else will ever know what you've done or the way in which you've done it. Even still, you'll know. Remember, you can't luck into becoming a champion, and you can't cheat the process. Today matters, so do what champions do, and be great right where you are.

Love the game. Tap into your passion, and keep your commitments.

Give your best. Don't let anything keep you from your maximum effort.

Overcome adversity. Be tough and resilient, no matter the circumstances.

Seek Improvement. See whatever happens today as an opportunity to learn, grow, and keep getting better.

Get coached. Stay humble and hungry.

Be a teammate. Make those around you better.

Take risks. Have the courage it takes to really, truly compete to win.

And choose a positive attitude. Live, work, and play with optimism. Don't forget, the best is yet to come.

ACKNOWLEDGMENTS

One thing writing a book has confirmed for me is that, like most positive or successful ventures in my life, I'm not capable of much without the inspiration and direction that I can confidently say only comes from God. I hope this book will continue to further His plan for my life and for the lives of others. Thank you to my wife, Jess, for your never-ending support of my work and for showing me every day what a great teammate looks like. I love you. Thanks to my kids – Aden, Owen, and Leah – for their daily inspiration and encouragement. I wrote this book for you (and for the other important kids in my life, too – Cove, Bella, and Elona). I hope it can challenge and encourage you to do the hard work it takes to become a champion in the most important areas of your life. Never stop chasing excellence! I love you more than you'll ever know. Thanks also to so many of my friends and family members who've offered support, in both words and actions, for my writing, and those whose work has inspired mine. Specifically to Jim Harshaw, for thoughts on getting tough. To Rob Bell, for emphasizing that no one gets there alone. And to Coach Bechler, for helping me make success a choice. Finally, a special word of thanks to Mike Kirschner for his feedback and encouragement throughout this book's development. Coach, you are a great leader and developer of football players and teams, but more importantly, a great leader and developer of people. Thanks for your powerful example.

TRAVIS DAUGHERTY served as a head high school basketball coach in the state of Indiana for 14 years, where his teams won nearly 200 games. He was honored as the Indiana Basketball Coaches Association Coach of the Year in 2008. In 2017, his first book, *The LENS: Raising a Champion Athlete and Man in Today's Myopic World,* was published and released. He is the founder and director of the Champions 101 workshop series for athletes, sports parents, and coaches, and also serves as Assistant Director and Leadership Development Speaker for Higher Level Father-Son Basketball Camps. He and his wife Jessica have three kids: Aden, Owen, and Leah. You can connect with Travis on Twitter @CoachTDaugherty.

Interested in bringing the message of *Hidden Talent* to your team, company, or organization? For details on keynote speaking, one-on-one or small group coaching, workshop opportunities and more, contact Travis via email at travis@travisdaugherty.com.

Other work by Travis Daugherty:

Your game plan
for raising a
Champion
in sports & in life!

Learn more at
www.thelensbook.com

Made in the USA
Las Vegas, NV
19 December 2020